# Tommy at Gommecourt

## Thomas James Higgins

Late 1/5 North Staffs Regiment

**CHURNET VALLEY BOOKS**
1 King Street, Leek, Staffordshire, ST13 5NW  01538 399033
www.leekbooks.co.uk
© Alan Henry Higgins and Churnet Valley Books 2005
ISBN 1 904546 27 7

# FOREWORD

Thomas James Higgins was a foundling, found in 1889 on the doorstep of a police sergeant named Higgins, in an expensive cot and fine clothes.

Police Sergeant Higgins discovered that a 'baby farmer' had fled to Stoke-on-Trent from the Reading area, with five babies, because the Reading police wanted to question her about the deaths of a number of children. Three of these five babies were found drowned in a canal, the fourth was never found, the fifth might have been Thomas.

Thomas was named by the police sergeant. He kept Thomas until he was about six and then he was put into various homes and workhouses, as Sergeant Higgins could not afford to keep him with six children of his own.

## My experience as a soldier in the British Army in the Great War

## Taken from a diary kept from 1914-1919

## What I have written here is true

Thomas Higgins
Late L/Cpl T. Higgins 201640
1/5 North Staffordshire Regt.
11 Platoon. C. Coy

# 1914 to 1915

I am writing this little book from notes taken at the time the incidents happened.

1914 to
May 1915

It really starts in August 1914. England had declared war upon Germany. Everybody was war mad. England was in the right, as Germany had broken her Treaties and overrun Belgium to attack France. Fiery speeches, banners waving, bands playing and a hysterical press, were urging men married or single to come and fight for England. The whole country resounded with the cry "Your King and Country need you".

I was working where I am working now, at Etruria Steel Works. Men were throwing their jobs up and enlisting, I caught the fever for it, and enlisted in the Infantry. They tried to get me to stay at work as so many had enlisted, and we were on war munitions, but I would go.

I enlist
May 1915

On May 26th 1915, I joined the 3/5 North Staffs Regiment. I met a chap named Jim Lloyd outside the Drill Hall and he enlisted at the same time, and we were always good pals. The 3/5 were stationed at Shelton. We were billeted at private houses. Jim Lloyd was put in the same billet, and the Government paid so much per head for our food. This was an emergency war measure, as the big camps up and down the country were only just being built,

There were two more in the same house who enlisted at the same time as I did. One was Robert Goodhill, he was, and still is a clerk at Pidducks Jewellers in Hanley. He was a swank. He never left England, he injured his ankle, and I heard that he became Sergeant Major in a Home Service Regt. - and never went out to go fight.

1915
Shelton
It was a very good billet we had at Shelton, plenty of good food and a hot bath any time we wanted one. I could have soldiered for the duration of the war here. For the first week or two we used to go drilling on Hanley Park. Then we started to go everyday to Wetley Common. We started at 8am in the morning and got back at about 4pm in the afternoon. We were taught trench digging and various kinds of drilling.

I got my first Army Crime marching from the Common. We had strict orders not to drink from our water bottles on the march, the idea was to make us hard in war, if we could not get much water. But we had only just left civil life, and it was a very hot day. I was just having a drink when Goodhill, who was now a Lance Corporal, saw me. He reported me to the O.C. Mr. W. H. Robinson who gave me two days C. B. I had to report every half hour at Stoke Drill Hall from 5:30 till 9:30pm for two nights.

While we were at Shelton we had four recruiting marches through the Potteries, Newcastle and Trentham. They took place on Saturdays, in June and July 1915.

1915
Recruiting
Marches

There were bands playing and the roads were lined with thousands of people who had come out to see Blizzard's Bold Brigade, as they called us after C.O. Col. Blizzard, and the following song was composed for the battalion. It was sung all over the Potteries at the time.

## Song of Battalion

Hark! Have you heard that war note
That thrilling trumpet call.
That soundeth out o'er Vale and Hamlet,
O'er hut, and Lordly Hall.
'Tis Mother England calling,
Her sons unto her aid.
Then up ye men of Staffordshire,
Join Blizzard's Bold Brigade.
Then up ye men of Staffordshire,
Join Blizzard's Bold Brigade.

There's glory in your banner,
There's music in that cheer
That rolls along the battle line
From men of Staffordshire.
From Himalay's summits,
To Minden's murky plain
Your Colours tell your story,
Unsmirched by blot or stain.
Your Colours tell your story,
Unsmirched by blot or stain.

Then Proudly speed the slogan
That starts from Trentham Hall,

And sweeps along the murmuring Trent
To distant Caverswall.
Desert be bench and workshop,
Bereft be wife and maid.
We'll die for dear old England,
In Blizzard's Bold Brigade
We'll die for dear old England,
In Blizzard's Bold Brigade.

And many a one did die before it was over, but of that more later. While I was at Shelton I was picked out one Monday in July to go to Stafford, about fifty of us altogether on a recruiting march. We went by train, and had a Scotch Pipe Band in front of us. We marched round the town, then had tea in the Shire Hall. We came back to Shelton at night.

1915
Hanley
Park Fetes

On the first Wednesday and Thursday in July it was Hanley Park Fetes. We had already dug trenches in the park, and we had a sham attack on the trenches, to give the civvies an idea of what it was like. I did not think that twelve months later I should be in an attack that was so awful I could not imagine anything so terrible.

1915
March
away from
Shelton

About July 29th 1915 we had orders to leave Shelton and proceed to Stafford. We had to march it with full pack and rifle, this is called Full Marching Order. Thousands of people came to see us start. My wife and Jim Lloyd's wife walked by our side into Stoke. Some blokes followed us as far as Trentham.

What a splendid day it was. While we were forming up to start from Stoke, the chaps were singing this:

> Only one more kit inspection
> Only one more church parade
> Only one more marching order
> Then we'll all go home again.
> We'll get our civvy clothes on
> Oh how happy we shall be
> When this blooming war is over
> No more soldiering for me.

July 1915
Arrive at
Stafford

This was sung to the tune of 'What a friend we have in Jesus'. We then said goodbye to our wives, mothers and sweethearts and with a sigh and a cheer marched off to the town of Stafford, 18 miles away. We got to Stone about dinner, had a meal and about an hours rest. Then we started off again, and reached Stafford about 5pm with church bells ringing, and the people in thousands lining the streets to give us a welcome. The Battalion was put up half in private houses, and half in schools. I was billeted in a house in Oxford Gardens. It was not so good as at Shelton but it was alright. We carried out our training on Stafford Common.

We had a night bivouacking on Cannock Chase. We marched to Cannock, and bivouacked. We had 2 poles, between four men about a yard long, to these we tied string, and made tents of two blankets, four men had to sleep under, on a blanket laid on the ground. The Colonel's idea was to show how you would have to camp for the night on a long march in warfare. It would have

August
1915
Bivouac at
Cannock

been alright if we had a rubber ground sheet to lie on, instead of a blanket. When the dew came down the blanket became damp, and we did not get much sleep all night. The next morning I got a good breakfast, we had got to find sticks to cook our own bacon. I had got some sticks over night and put them under my pack to keep them dry. Some of the others gave me their bacon, before they would go to the trouble to find wood. We were going back to Stafford after breakfast, so they only missed one meal. I don't know how some of them would have gone on if we had got to camp for two or three days. We broke camp after breakfast. As we were leaving the Chase it came on to rain, and it rained all the way to Stafford about 6 miles away. We were soaked when we got back to billet. We thought it was hard times, but the times were coming when we couldn't get dry for weeks, we were young soldiers yet, and didn't know what we had to go through in the future.

August
1915
Life at
Stafford

We made friends with almost everybody in Stafford. I was billeted along with a chap named Hulme, from Tunstall, he was a good piano player and singer. I could also do a song or two. When we went in a public house he would get on the piano and sing and I would do a song. Then the civvies would treat us and send the hat round. At weekends we were never short of beer.

The landlord at the George and Dragon took me and Hulme round the Salt Works at Stafford. The salt is drawn from brine springs. The vats are always on the boil and as the water evaporates the salt is left in the vat. The salt is then put in square wooden moulds. It is then turned out in those blocks that come round on carts, that you see in Hanley. After we had been round the Salt Works, we were very dry with seeing so much salt about, so we adjourned to the George and Dragon for a drink.

We had been stationed at Stafford about three weeks, when I got a weekend's pass to come home. I felt as though I had been away for years, as I had never been away from home before. I was pleased to see my wife and little son Tommy again. My brother-in-law Jack Clarke was home on leave at the same time. He was in the Bedford Regiment. This was the last time I saw Jack till the end of the War.

I got back to Stafford by Monday morning. It was our turn to go to the schools. They were in Corporation Street. This was where we started to soldier properly. We were sleeping on boards with rough blankets, and eating army cooking. We thought once again, what a rough life. But there came a time later when I would have given years of my life for those same boards, blankets and Army food.

We stayed at Stafford until about the middle of September 1915. Then the Battalion had orders to go to a big camp at Grantham in Lincolnshire. On the Saturday before we left Stafford, Col Blizzard took 3 Companies to the Potteries, for a last recruiting march. Companys A, B,

September
1915
I take
French
Leave

& C went and they came back to Stafford on Tuesday morning. D Coy, the one I was in was left at the Schools at Stafford to do guards, but before 2pm the same day, at least half of our Coy had taken French leave. I along with four pals slipped out of the schools just as Bob Goodhill, who was now a sergeant, came to warn us for duty. We walked to Stone, through Sandon. At the villages we put one of the lads in the middle of the four as though we were on escort duty, so that the police would not stop us and ask to see our pass. We got on the train at Stone, and were at Stoke as soon as the 3 companies.

September
1915 Find
wife very
ill

When I got home I had a shock. I thought how glad the wife would be to see me, but I found her very ill in bed, in great pain, and the doctor attending her. I stopped the weekend and got back to Stafford on Tuesday morning, at the same time as the other Coys. I got through without paying my fare, by mixing up with those who had been allowed to go. About dinner hour you should have seen the parade to face the C. O. About half the D Coy had been absent. I told the Colonel I had been to see the wife who was ill. So the punishment I got was pay stopped. He phoned to Dr Swain to see if it was true. He gave all the others Pack Drill as well.

September
1915
Arrive at
Grantham

All the people of Stafford seemed to turn out to see us off to Grantham on the Thursday. When we got there we had a march right out of Grantham, to a place called Belton Park 3 miles away. The camp was composed of huts and there were thousands of soldiers here in training. This was where we did some real soldiering, drilling all day. Then they had us out at night trench attacking, and long route marches. We also did our range firing here.

On September 21st 1915 I had a telegram from my mother in law, saying that my wife was very ill after an operation in the Infirmary. Could I come home to see her. I got a special leave after a lot of trouble, and came with another man whose child was dead. We got to Nottingham about 9pm and found we could not get a train to Stoke till morning. My mate had some friends in Bulwell, close to, so we went there and stayed the night. We caught the first train next morning and I got in Hanley at 9am. I went straight off to the Infirmary to see Lizzie. I found her very ill. I went again in the afternoon and again at night. I had got to go back to Camp the next day, but I went to see Lizzie before I went. It was awful to see my loved one lying there so ill and to go away miles off and not see her. How that parting hurt. She looked so weak and helpless lying there. But I was a soldier now and I had to go. When I got to Nottingham, I had to wait 2 hours for a train. So I had a look around the town. I got back at Grantham at night - I remember it was pouring with rain, and I got wet through going to the camp. A parcel my poor old mother had given me, of some cake and tobacco, was spoilt.

It was the end of November before I got another leave. I was longing to see the wife again, as she was better now, and I was getting home sick. How I enjoyed that leave. My little Tommy had grown nicely. That weekend fairly flew and I was back at Grantham on Monday morning. The Battalion sent the first draft of men to France now. The 1/5 North Staffs had been smashed up in an attack at Hulloch so our battalion made them up again.

Christmas
Day
1915
At
Grantham

Christmas Day 1915 came. I was still at Grantham. Col Blizzard did his best to make us happy. He gave us a grand feed, and there seemed to be everything. Turkey, and Sausages, Roast Beef, Pork and Fowl, and Plum Pudding. Then there were beer and minerals. In fact it was a grand Spread altogether. The Officers acted as waiters. Among the Officers who served us was Major Boote, Lieuts Watkin, Chapman, Robinson and Bowers. These men were all killed at Foncquevillers on July 1st the following year. Also Capt Wilton he was killed at Bocquoy in March 1917.

December
1915
Home on
Leave

The next day, Boxing Day, I was on fatigue duty carrying plates and bowls back to stores, when I and a lot more men were told to go to Company Headquarters to see the Officer in Charge as we had got to go on six days leave. We could hardly believe it, but when we got there we were told, as we had finished our firing, we might have to go to France any day, so we were allowed six days leave in case of going out suddenly.

# 1916

I enjoyed that leave. I came to Hanley with a chap named Jack Regan. I was bottled up when I got home. Then I found my wife at my mother's and I stayed there till morning. I met Jack every day and we had a fine time. I had to start back for camp on New Years Eve 1915. As me and Jack were going through Grantham twelve o'clock was striking and the new year was with us. I said to Jack, "I wonder where we shall be this time next year". He answered, "Oh merry and bright somewhere." Poor chap, he was dead before next year. He was killed at Gommecourt July 1st 1916.

February 1916 Vaccination Leave

I was still at Grantham at the end of January. When they vaccinated all of us who were ready for France they gave us four days sick leave for home. I was glad to get home again to see the wife. I over stayed this time by 2 days. To get out of bother I sent a telegram to the C. O. saying my wife was ill. A policeman came to see if it was true. It was alright, so I got 2 days extension. I went back on the Sunday night. The wife came with me to Stoke Station. I said to her, "This is my last leave, kiss me good-bye dear." She said, "Not it, I shall soon see you again", but she was wrong. It was three years before we met once more.

February
1916
At Long
Eaton

When I got to Grantham along with a chap named Tom Perry, we found out the Battalion had moved and gone to Long Eaton close to Derby. The Notts and Derbys were in our huts. We lay down till morning on the Guard Room floor. Then we got a Railway Warrant from their C. O. and went to Long Eaton on the Monday. It was a nice little place and we enjoyed our stay there. We were billeted in what had been a big lace mill. When I was walking out after Church Parade, the following Sunday a gentleman stopped me, and asked if I should like to come to his house for dinner, as it would be better than Army food. I accepted his kind invitation, and stayed for tea and supper. He told me to come any time for a bit of a meal. I went there every Sunday while I was there. He was a manager at a lace mill. He took me and showed me round the mill one day. While at Long Eaton I was in a military funeral for the first time in my life. I was one of the firing party over the grave. There were thousands of people in that cemetery that day. This took place about three days before I went to France. We had been here about five weeks, and then Col Blizzard gave about 250 of us a farewell supper.

Then on Saturday March 25th 1916, we entrained for Southampton, en route for France. Jim Lloyd, of whom I have spoken before, came out at the same time. We got to Southampton at about 4 o'clock in the afternoon. Then we marched to a canvas camp about three miles away. I went down to Southampton at night. It is a fine town. From here I sent Lizzie word that I was going to France. We stayed in the tents, Saturday and Sunday. On Monday morning, we marched down to the docks and here we were served out with new rifles and bayonets. Then we went in what are called the embarkation sheds, until about 5pm. Then we went on board a ship called Edward VII.

We set sail about dusk. They packed us on that ship like herrings in a barrel as there were men from all regiments as well as us going out. We were given a pound tin of bully beef and three biscuits that took a hammer to break them. This was our rations until the end of our journey. How they got a 1000 men on the boat, God knows. As I said there were other regimental drafts besides ours. We could not stand properly for the packs we carried. And we could not sit or lie down. When, after an almost super human struggle to get your pack off, you lost it in the crush.

When we were just out of the harbour, a violent storm met us. The ship seemed to be tossed about like a cork. Men were sea sick all over the place. I stayed in one place and tried to sleep. I wasn't sea sick which was a wonder, as I was rolled all over the place and packs were rolling about on top of us. When we got half way across the Channel we thought our last day had come. The boat seemed to stand on end and spin round. Then the engines broke down. We had to be towed back to Southampton. We got in about daybreak and got off the ship again. They took us a march round the sea front, and we needed it. We were cramped up after a night like we had just been through.

As it was still too rough on Tuesday night to sail, they put us in the sheds to stay for a night. We had to lie on the bare floors, with only our overcoats to cover us. The night was bitterly cold as the breezes came sweeping over us from the sea. Sleep was impossible. We were also short of food, as the rations we had been served out were gone. We asked the officer about some more. He said he had served out all he was allowed, to troops going over to France. We still had tea and sugar but it was a big task to get hot water to brew it. Some of the seamen were selling hot water at threepence a cup. This is how men were treated who were just going out to risk their lives for their Country. I think it was a shame. After a hungry cold and sleepless night, we were taken another march on Wednesday morning. As we marched along, the men were breaking ranks and dodging into shops buying bread. I was unlucky - I had no money so I did not get any. Then the Officer stopped the march and we returned to the sheds. There we had a lecture, telling us how bad it looked buying bread and breaking the ranks. People would think we were starving. And we must remember we were soldiers; by Heavens, we could not forget it.

March
1916
Off to
France

In the evening of the same day, Wednesday March 29th 1916, we embarked on another boat called the Belle France. We were packed again like sardines in a box, but it was a splendid night, so I stayed on deck the whole night. The sea was as calm as a lake all the way across. You could see the searchlights from the warships playing round the skies and over the waters - it was a grand sight. Our ship had no lights showing owing to submarines, and we all had life belts on, in case of being sunk. As I stood on deck, and watched the lights of Southampton fade, I took my last look on Old England. Oh the thoughts that came to me at those few moments. I thought of home, my wife and son, and when, if I ever should, see the loved faces again. We all knew that some of us would never see our homes again. But Fate will be.

March
1916
Up the
Seine

We got to Le Havre at about 6am on Thursday morning. Then we sailed up the river Seine. Oh the beauties of that trip up the river, the villages dotted about in black and white and all colours, was finer than any picture.

March
1916
Rouen

We got to Rouen about 2pm where the boat stopped. It seemed strange to be standing on deck of a ship at the quay side and taking our first look at a French city. The French people were passing to and fro, as though unaware that British soldiers existed. We were glad to land if only to stretch our legs once more. We then had a long march, nearly all up hill, through the city to a big canvas camp on a race course. There was plenty to interest us, although the sun beat down and we were boiling with sweat. Everything we saw seemed new and strange to us. We got to camp about 5pm. We were then put into tents, as many men as they could cram into one. Then they gave us our tea. How thankful we were for that meal. We had some bread and butter. I never thought bread tasted so good. It was the first bread since Monday morning, and it was now Thursday night.

Next morning March 31st we were paraded for a Medical Inspection to see if we were fit for the front. This was the manner of it. About 200 men, as naked as they were born, in two long lines about two yards apart. Each line face to face. The doctor walked down between the lines, if he noticed anyone looking very ill he wasn't fit. The rest he passed as fit. In the afternoon, I drew my first pay in French money. A five franc note, worth 3s. 7d in our money. On Saturday April 1st we went and fired on the range, then we had the afternoon off to lounge about the camp.

Sunday April 2nd we had a Church Parade. The service took place in a big Y.M.C.A. hut in the camp. This was the last Church Parade I had for some time.

Monday April 3rd we were taken on a great sandy plain drilling all day. Every time the wind blew the sand nearly choked us. We had dinner out consisting of one potato and a piece of meat, which we cooked ourselves over bits of stick. I saw for the first time some of the punishments on active service. Three men who had been out before, tried to get away at Southampton. They were caught, and came over with us. There they were, in the glare of the sun tied to a wheel of a gun, arms outstretched as though on a cross. It gave me a shudder at the time, but I saw a lot of this in France later on.

April
1916
Training
at Rouen

Tuesday April 4th we were drilling and live bomb throwing. At night we had a practice night attack on some trenches - we were out the greater part of the night. Wednesday 5th drilling again. Thursday 6th another night stunt as well. They were making us fed up. Friday 7th morning drill, in the afternoon pay once more. During the week it was a scramble for food, you were lucky when you got it.

April
1916
A visit to
Town of
Rouen

On Saturday April 8th I got a pass to go down to the town. I had a good look round. Some of the places you went in for a drink, had women in Eve's costume. It was strange to English eyes. I should have been in camp by 9pm, but did not get in till turned 10 o'clock. I should have been punished for this, if I had been stopping in camp, but we had to start for the front the next day. I had my first letter from England that Saturday morning containing a photo of my wife and son Tommy. I carried this photo with me right to the end of the War.

On Sun April 9th had orders to start for the Front.

April 9th
1916
Start for
Front

It took us all morning to get served out with all the things we had got to take with us. This is a list of them, all to be carried on us: pack containing overcoat, shirt and pants, socks & shaving kit; rifle and 150 rounds of ammunition; haversack containing 1lb of bully beef and biscuits; equipment with entrenching tool and shaft, and bottle of water; 1 ground sheet; 1 rainproof cloak; 1 fur coat; and 2 gas helmets. This load we carried to the station three miles away. We were almost dropping when we got there. We were then packed into carriages until we could hardly move to take our loads off. We started on our trip, one that lasted 24 hours. That train journey beats everything. We should dash along for a bit, then go dead slow for a bit longer. This was the same all the way through the ride. The chaps were getting out and walking, and catching the train up when it stopped, but all things have an end, even a ride in a trench train.

April
1916
Aubigny

On Monday April 10th in the afternoon, we got to a place called Aubigny. This was the nearest railhead to the firing line. Now we could hear the roar of the guns for the first time. It was just like continuous thunder. There were aeroplanes up in the air, being shelled by the Germans. It was a sight to see the shells bursting all round the planes, but I got used to sights like these later, and I saw many a plane both English and German, fetched down. The airmen of those days were heroes on both sides.

We then had a stiff march to a little village named Equarve, here we stopped.  It was a village close to the firing line, just behind Neuville St. Vaast.  Here the 1/5 North Staffs were holding the line.  I shall not forget my first night in such surroundings.  We lay on bare earth floors, with only our top coats to cover us.  The weather in the north of France was bitterly cold.  What with the hard ground, the cold and the roar of the cannon I got no sleep, tired as I was.  The night was one of misery.  Later I was to know these were good quarters to where I slept many times afterwards.  At last we were tasting the joys of soldiering.

The next day we were taken a long march to buck us up.  In the afternoon we had gas helmet drill.  After tea up, we could do what we liked until roll call 9.30pm.  I thought I could do a drink, so I went in an estaminet, or pub.  I called for beer, a glass cost a penny.  That was three farthing too much, it was awful.  I saw soldiers drinking a red wine.  I found it was a franc a bottle, so I had one.  To my surprise it tasted sour.  I saw the others enjoying it.  Theirs was sweet, mine was sour.  The secret lay in the fact if you asked for Vin Rouge, you got it sour.  For another 2d you had some bitron, a very sweet liqueur, mixed with the wine and it tasted like port.

While at Equarve I had my first view of the Firing Line.  I climbed a big hill at night and on the hill was the village of Mt. St. Eloi.  We were not allowed there in

April
1916
I see the
Firing
Line

daylight, as it was in view of the Germans. In fact we were not supposed to go there at all. The village was in ruins. The Germans held it in 1914 and the French lost 7,000 men in driving them back to Neuville St. Vaast. I went in a ruined church there, a picture of desolation. Statues smashed, half the roof off. The confessional, a big heap of broken wood. Shell holes were everywhere. A strange thing was that a big picture of the Crucifixion was almost undamaged. Then outside I looked on the war front, it was dark by now. What a sight it was. I can hardly describe it. The line seemed to be in front and all round me. Lights of all colours were going up in hundreds. Then the roar of cannon, the rattle of machine guns; in fact where I stood bullets were whizzing all round me. But I was blind to danger, I was so taken with the grand but terrible sight before me. I could see shells bursting in the air and on the ground until the earth seemed to tremble. I wondered how it was possible for human beings to live among such an inferno. Then I thought this is what the civilisation of the present day has brought us to. "Hell of Man's own making". Then I went back to my billet and slept in spite of the hard ground, the cold, and roaring cannon.

April
1916
At
Neuville
St. Vaast

The next night we were sent on fatigue up to the trenches, carrying rations and barbed wire. As we started off it began to rain, and it rained all night. We got to St. Vaast drowned out. The trenches ran through the town. It had been a fairly large town before the war, but now was a heap of ruins. The shells were crashing everywhere. When we got back to billet, tired out and wet through, we threw ourselves down to rest. Oh for the comforts of home and a good fire just then.

April
1916
At
Schellers

The Battalion was recalled from that part a few days later. Then we went on what was called Divisional rest. We set off marching April 20th landing about 4pm at a village named Schellers. Here we slept the night in old barns. It was heaven to sleep on some old straw. Off again next day to a place called Marquay. Here we were to stop a bit. We were hot and thirsty and there was a rush for water. We found only one well in the village and the kindly Frenchies had taken the rope and handle off, so we were drinking water out of stinking pools to quench our thirst. We were billeted again in barns. The one our platoon was in was alive with rats. They climbed the walls and beams and dropped on us as we slept. But we soon got used to rats. You get used to anything in time if you have to stick it long enough. We stayed during Easter 1916 and I received a parcel from home with some homemade cake in it on Easter Monday.

The town of St. Pol was only 4 miles off, so me and Arthur Lomas, a pal, got a pass to go there one afternoon to have a look round. When we got there we found we had not much time to look round, as we had to be back by 8.30pm. I changed a postal order mother had sent me.

April
1916
I visit St.
Pol

Then we started cussing because we had not stayed in the billet like the others and had a rest, instead of walking our legs off. While at Marquay we had an all-day route march - we took the cookers with us, and had dinner on the way. We marched about 20 miles that day. I was completely tired out when I got back. On April 30th we were all inoculated and we had a day's sick rest that day.

May 1916
On the
march

On May 3rd we started for the trenches again. The first day we got to a place named Bienvillers. It was a hot day for marching and I was soaked through with sweat. I think the rats in the barn the platoon was in were worse than Marquay. They came and sneaked your food from beside you. Still as I said before we soon thought little of that. All the trenches and dugouts we found were literally swarming with them. At Monchy a place we came to later on, a man was killed one night and we put him in a bit of a shelter, and put a guard over him. When we came to take him out next morning his face was almost eaten away by rats. They were nearly as big as cats, and they would stand and face you.

May 1916
Going in
Firing
Line

We left Bienvillers the next morning. As we got closer to the line we had to stay in a wood till dusk owing to shelling. Then we reached a place called St. Amand, about nightfall. We went to the trenches which were close to, on May 5th. They were at a place called Foncquevillers, the north part of the Somme. Our platoon No. 11 and C Coy were put in the support trenches just

behind the fire trench.  Here I had my first night in a dugout.
This was a cave dug out of the ground, and propped up with
baulks of wood.  You could hear shells and trench mortars
dropping and exploding outside.  But none dropped on our
dug out, or I should not be writing this, as it was only about
3 feet deep.  Still this was one of the chances of war.

May 1916
In the
Trenches

The next day we had to take over the front line
trench.  At last I was in the thick of it.  I now did my first
turn as day sentry on the firing step.  We had to look
through a periscope set up in the side of the trench.  With
this you could see without being seen yourself.  I had my
first look at the German trenches.  They were about a 100
yards away and seemed a mass of thick barbed wire.  It
was sudden death to put your head over the top in
daylight, as the German snipers were crack shots.  At
night you had to look over, and watch for Jerry coming on
raids.  You had to risk the bullets that came over all the
time from rifles and machine guns.  An amusing thing
happened the first day in, although we did not think it so
at the time.  The dinner was cooked in a dug out at the
back, and sent down to the front trench in a dixie.  They
were just dishing it out to us when Jerry dropped a shell
on the side of the trench and filled the bully stew with dirt.
So we got no dinner that day.  As times went on we saw a
lot more meal times than meals.

After a few days in the fire trench, we went in
support to the village of Foncquevillers, where the

trenches started from.  We were in cellars in day time, as the village was under fire as much as the trenches with shells and bullets.  The church was a ruin.  It was a proper death trap.  We had to pass it to get to the trenches.  He used to drop shells there all the time as well as sweep the place with machine guns.  The tower with the date 1630 was still standing - it was about all that was left.  The graveyard was smashed up with bones and coffins of those who had lain there for years scattered all about by explosions of shells.

I now had my first job over the top in "No Mans Land".  This was the ground between the German trenches and ours.  Me and Arthur Lomas were put on covering party for some men who were putting barbed wire in front of our trench.  We had to go out and lie about 20 yards in front of them to give them warning if Jerry was coming over.  Things went on alright despite bullets and we got in without loss.  I had the same job for the next three nights and Arthur Lomas with me as we had become great pals.  After a week of this we went in trenches at the back.  These were called Fort Dick.  Here our rations were very scarce.  A 2lb loaf for 6 and 1lb of bully for 4 men.  Here Lomas used to say, when rations were shorter than usual, "Buck up, Jerry's starving and so are we".

I came under my first heavy bombardment here. Fritz started one night with trench mortars, shells and

May 1916
Under
Bombard-
ment

machine gun fire. The air was alive with mortars and shells. It seemed to be raining fire. When our guns opened fire too, the noise and roar made the earth tremble. We thought Fritz was coming over. Our Battalion Major was in the trenches, and someone passed the word down, "The Major has the wind up". Someone told him. He said, "Pass it back, I'm not the only mother's son with the wind up tonight". It was like being in the midst of a fiery volcano, thinking how long you would last. Then the bombardment stopped as suddenly as it had began. The day was just breaking, everything seemed so still after the fierce tumult. Then the birds began to sing as they greeted the new day, and it made me think of that ages old saying "Peace on Earth, and Goodwill towards Men". There were many men killed that night.

Then we went out of the trenches, to a village behind called Bienvillers au Bois. It was very close to the line but had not been knocked about as much as Foncquevillers. It was still full of civvies, people who would not leave their homes until they fell on top of them. I had a look at a French cemetery here. The tombs were like greenhouses of glass over where the grave was. The wreaths were all beads and artificial flowers. There was a crucifix on almost every grave, some had photos of the person who was buried there. If it happened to be a soldier, sailor or policeman buried there, the caps or

May 1916
Leave the
Trenches

helmets were placed on the grave as well. It was an interesting place to visit. It looked so peaceful and pretty. I visited here again in March 1917 but what a different scene it was - the tombs were shattered and the graves ploughed open by shells. A scene of wreck and ruin. Such is War.

May 1916
On the
march

After one night at Bienvillers we had a night march to a place called Sus. St. Leger. Oh that march; after being in the trenches and getting no proper sleep, we were quite done up. I am sure I marched the last mile or two with my eyes shut.

May 1916
At Sus St.
Leger

It was Sunday morning when we got here. It turned out to be a pretty village, we thought we had come out for a rest. What hopes. After a day or two to get the mud of the trenches cleaned off us, we were set to digging trenches close to a wood. These were the exact reproduction of those we had just left, and the wood represented Gommecourt Wood that the Germans held. After this we started practicing an attack we were to make on the Gommecourt front in the Somme Offensive. We were out at day break every morning doing this, till 10am with smoke bombs, and gas helmets on. Then after breakfast we went in a wood making hurdles for the trenches in bad weather. We were at this for a fortnight out at daybreak 'til 5pm. Still we looked back upon it as a happy time because we had the evening to ourselves and we used to have a concert troupe giving us concerts. I had my first pay at Sus St. Leger on May 22nd. It was 10 Francs, the biggest pay I'd had out here. Arthur Lomas said we will have a rich man's drink for once. So we had a bottle or two of Champagne - it was about 3 francs a bottle in France.

June 3rd we left Sus St. Leger, and went back to Bienvillers. We were at the other end of the village this time. It was pretty well in ruins here. I found out after that this village was under 1,000 yard from Fritz's front line. We were put in an old barn with hardly any roof on it. About this time it started to rain heavy and it kept on almost every day and night until the end of June. Then we had it rough. We started to dig trenches to attack Fritz from. Every evening at dusk we went up a trench which ran from Bienvillers to Foncquevillers. With it raining so heavy, this trench was half full of water. Still we had to use it as the road was swept by shells and bullets. After going along this trench we were soaked through to the waist. When we got to the line we had to dig support and communication trenches under machine gun and shell fire. We lost a few men every night on this. We generally got back to Bienvillers next morning wet through, and dead beat. When we came to lie down the floor of the barn was a mass of mud, where it rained in. Our overcoats which we put over us, were wet through. We went to sleep wet and awoke wet. It was worse than a dog's life. At midday we had to parade for inspection of rifles, shaved and

June 1916
Leave St.
Leger

At
Bienviller
s

cleaned up. In the afternoons, we were put to digging narrow trenches all around Bienvillers for the civil population to get in when Fritz was shelling heavy. A Frenchman went round with a bell warning the people to leave before the Battle of the Somme started. But a great many would not leave. At one house an old couple had two coffins to put them in if they got killed. This will show how people cling to their homes.

June
1916
Fall
Sick

For days now I had suffered with an abscess under my teeth. I was almost mad with pain. My face was so swollen, my right eye was nearly closed. I went to the Medical Officer two or three days together, but I still had to work on it. What with the pain and the conditions we were working under, and only sleeping when I was completely exhausted, I wished I was dead many a time. At last the M.O. sent me in an ambulance to a first aid depot. Here I slept in a tent on stretchers with a blanket. I thought it like heaven. After a night I was put in a motor ambulance and sent to Lucheux, some 10 miles away. Here a dentist drew two teeth and seemed to pull the top of my head off doing it. But I got some relief from pain after it.

June 1916
At
Bienvillers

Then I was sent back to Bienvillers. We did a few more nights trench digging before we marched back to Sus St. Leger again. We were only there for 2 days to practice the attack over again. Then we marched off, this time for Foncquevillers. A and B Coys along with South

Staffords were put in the fire trench. D and C Coys - I was in C - were put in the cellars.

June 1916<br>Digging<br>Advance<br>Trench

The next night C Coy had to find a big covering party for the 6th North Staffs, as they had got to dig an advance trench between our front line and Jerry's front line. I was in the covering party that was nearly 100 strong. We crawled out in "No Mans Land" until we were about 20 yards away from the German trenches. We then lay down stretched in a long line, with our heads to Jerry. Each man was 3 yards apart. The trench diggers were about 20 yards behind us. Where I lay we could hear Fritz putting wire out. I'm sure he heard our chaps digging, they made such a noise as there were such a lot of them. Still not a shot came over. He was biding his time. We got in after that night with no loss.

June 1916<br>Discovered<br>by the<br>Enemy

The next night, it would be about June 23rd, we went out again. We got to our positions of the night before. The 6th North started their digging. The night was pitch black and it was raining heavily. Fritz waited until we had settled down. Then we heard a German rifle fire four or five shots rapid on the extreme right of us. Another one answered on the left. We heard a loud shout in German. Then Hell and all its fury broke loose over us. He rained trench mortars on those who were digging. Shells in hundreds were dropped on our trenches. On us, the covering party, they turned dozens of machine guns. He got our range just right. The bullets came like

June 1916
Under
Fire

streams of water from hose pipes. You could hear them cutting the grass as they came. I felt them pounding in the earth round my head, and shoulders, and all round me. The roar of guns, the loud explosions of mortars, the horrible shrieks and the screams of the wounded and dying men were awful to hear. The terrible horror of that night is impossible to describe. My mate was riddled with bullets at the first discharge. He soon died. We lay with our faces pressed in the wet grass, and wondered how many more seconds of life were left to us. We mentally said good-bye to this world and prepared for the next. If I had got to die that night, I prayed for a quick death, and not to be smashed and mangled like some of the poor chaps around me, dying in agony.

June 1916
Under
Fire

During a lull in the firing you could hear the terrible cries of dying men. It seemed more unnerving than the screams of shells and bullets. I spoke to the chaps on either side of me, one answered, one was dead. I crawled a bit closer to the German trenches, and lay close to his wire in a hollow, and his machine guns fired over me from this position. I was safe for a short time. Then our trench mortars opened out and began to drop in his wire. Then I was in danger of being blown to bits. When I rushed back to where I came from most of the men close to me were dead now. I should have been dead as well, if I had not got under his wire, they were riddled with bullets. The Germans were slacking off a bit now.

The covering party had orders to fall back on the advance trench. That is what was left of us, which was not many. This was about 4 foot deep in places, and in others not above a foot deep. It was almost half full of water from the heavy rain.

June 1916
My Pal
Killed

Here I saw the last in this world of poor Arthur Lomas, they were just getting him in. He was a mass of blood and mud, and he died as soon as they got him in. The remains of the covering party were told to hold the advance trench till daylight, which was not far off now. There we stood up to knees and waists in water in this bit of trench, expecting Fritz to come over to us at any moment. Then daylight came, and what a sight it revealed to our eyes. There in No Mans Land lay the bodies of those who had been in the covering party. In the trench where we stood were men lying about smashed by shells and mortars, mutilated beyond description.

June 1916
Getting
Back

Then we had orders to get back to our front line. We had to crawl in the mud like snakes on our bellies. Not one of us expected to get there alive, as the communication trench was only about six inches deep in places and we had to crawl over dead bodies all the way. All this time the bombardment from both sides was raging, and this didn't cease until after the Somme Battle that started July 1st. Fritz could see us getting back, but he contented himself by only taking pot shots at us, and wounding one or two men. We got back to the old cellar in Foncquevillers again amid the crash of the guns.  There we were served out with a tot of rum, and we began to take heart again.  They called a roll and found only about 30 of the covering party left.  The 46th Division, which we belonged to, lost over 1,000 men that night.

Under Bombard-ment in No Mans Land

After a sleep during the day, I, along with some more, were on covering party again.  The biggest bombardment of the war up to then was on now.  We shook hands all round with our mates before we went, as none of us expected to come back alive.  The rain was still falling and the trenches were full of water; I had to hold my rifle up to keep the bolt out of the water.  We got out on No Mans Land, the mortars and shells were dropping everywhere. The line of dead bodies we had left the night before were plain to see, owing to the Verey lights going up in all directions.  We crawled out to them and lay down among them.

1916 A Narrow Escape

A youth from Stoke named Reg Goodwin came with me and we were talking to one another, as with the roar of guns Fritz could not hear us.  We lay about 3 yards apart.  All of a sudden there was a rush of wind and a thud that shook the earth.  Me and Reg were almost blinded by earth and stones.  We knew what had happened; a shell had dropped right between us.  I lay with every nerve taut waiting to be blown to bits, but no explosion came.  After what seemed to be an age, my mate spoke.  "Higgins, it's a bloody dud", and so it was.

We could see the top of it sticking out of the ground. Death was cheated once more by a fraction.

We got back to our cellar with small losses and got down to sleep. But we were rudely awakened during the day. The cellar was soaking and full of fumes. The screams and shrieks of mangled men were terrible. A 9.2 shell had dropped down the stairway right in to the cellar and exploded. It blew about 4 men absolutely to bits. Of one man named Swetman, who happened to be sitting on the cellar steps at the time, all we found was his pay book. There were 8 killed and about 10 badly wounded. Blood and limbs and pieces of flesh were all over the cellar, it was like a shambles. I was covered with dust but unhurt.

We were out on covering party again that night. I remember Fritz was machine gunning very bad night and me and Goodwin pulled one or two of the dead bodies in front of us to stop the bullets - this is how callous war makes a man. Still self preservation is the first law of nature and I found it so many times in this war.

About June 27th we went to a village called Humbercamps. There was an 18 inch naval gun here. The first time they fired it the wind it made blew some old barns down like a pack of cards. We were here for a couple of days rest before our attack on Gommecourt. The day after we had an inspection by Major Wenger. I had my name taken because I hadn't got all the mud off my clothes.

June 1916
The
Colonel's
Speech

Not bad after what we had just been through. On the evening of June 30th we fell in to march up to Foncquevillers. The Colonel, Lieut-Col Burnett, made a short speech before we started. "Well Boys", he said, "By sunrise tomorrow morning I hope to see you on the other side of Gommecourt Wood." By that time or soon after, he was dead. Then the whole Battalion started to sing that well known hymn, "God be with you till we meet again". I have never heard that hymn sung with so much meaning as it was sung that evening, by men who were going to face death in all its most terrible forms. Whenever I hear that song now I think of that scene. The setting sun, the men with heads bowed thinking of those so dear to them. Many who sang that night, in a few short hours their voices were stilled for ever.

July 1st
1916
Going up
to go over

We got to Foncquevillers late in the night. We were told the 6th North were going over the top first and we were to follow them with picks shovels and barbed wire. These were to strengthen the position when we got there. Then we filed into a trench at the rear of the front line. This was up to the knees in water and here we stood and waited for daylight. When they came to serve our platoon out with rum, they found out someone had pinched it. So we got none. We stood there in the water with our teeth chattering with cold. As daylight grew stronger our intense bombardment opened out, it seemed as though all the artillery in the British army were gathered on our front. The din was terrific. This kept up for about an hour. Then it suddenly stopped. The 6th North should have gone over then, but Fritz rained such an awful shower of shells, mortars and bullets, that hardly a man got to his lines. We then had orders to advance.

July 1st
1916
Battle of
Gommecourt

In the trench leading to the front line, the sights I saw are impossible to properly describe. The trenches were literally running with blood. The dead and dying lay in heaps at the bottom of the trench. We had to climb over them as we went on. The shells were bursting everywhere, overhead, in front, and behind us Fritz was blowing our trenches flat. The barbed wire I was carrying kept getting entangled in broken wires and falling in the broken trench. I was cursing like mad over it.

July 1st
1916 In the
trenches

The Officer, Mr Bowers from Caverswall, said, "Let me carry part of it for you. I said, "Thank you sir." He took the iron stakes off me. Soon after a shell burst over us and killed him and I nearly fell on top of him. We were losing men fast. They were falling in front and behind, and we were walking on bodies all the way because with Fritz blowing the trenches about they were so narrow. Then a Mr Robinson from Newcastle took charge and led us to the advance trench, by this time I had thrown the spade and barbed wire away. The advance trench was nearly flat. As we turned into the trench we met Col Burnett and Capt Fletcher of C. Coy. It was the last I saw of them - they were both killed there a few minutes later.

July 1st
1916
Death all
around

At last we got to the jumping off place, with about half the number of men who started. In this trench was the same scenes of blood and death. I should think in about 1 hour over 600 men had been killed and wounded in the trenches alone. The 6th North was practically wiped out when we got to them. We rested a second or two, then came the order.

July 1st
1916 Over
the Top

"Fix Bayonets." The bullets were zipping just over the top of the trench and in No Mans Land whiz bangs and shells were bursting in hundreds. No one expected to come back again. The Officer yelled at the top of his voice: "One. Two. Three." Over we went with the best of luck. The man next to me named Chorlton fell back with a bullet in his head as he was springing over. I was more lucky, I got over with one spring, and there we were in a long line, rushing forward like mad men, to kill, or be killed. The line did not last for long. Men were falling like skittles bowled over. Some would sink down in a heap, others would shout and throw their hands up and totter forward a pace or two then fall face downwards never to rise again. The last one I saw was the Officer Robinson firing his pistol like mad, then he went down. I was close to Fritz's wire now. I could see them throwing bombs over the wire at us. Then there was a flash and I felt a fearful bang in my back and down I went among his smashed up wire. When I recovered myself I had a bad pain in my back. I felt there and found my equipment tunic and shirt ripped open, but strange to say only a scratch on my back, but it was very sore. It must have been a piece of shell that hit me flat, and knocked me out. If it had hit me edgeways it must have broken my back.

Then I looked about me and saw the awful position I was in. I shall never forget that Saturday, July 1st 1916, if I live to be a hundred  Shells were dropping close to me choking me with fumes and dirt. I soon found another danger - Fritz was riddling any poor devil he saw moving with bullets. I moved once and some bullets whizzed past just missing my head. I lay still after that with barbed wire sticking in me, I dare not move. That awful day seemed a life time to me. No more men came after us as the Division had not many left. If the Germans had made a counter attack, they would have easily taken our lines then.

Now the sun began to get high up, and I was parched with thirst, my water bottle had been knocked off somehow coming over. The smell of blood and dead bodies was sickening. I mentally said goodbye to those I loved, as I did not seem to have the ghost of a chance of living through that day. At last exhaustion was too much for me and amid all that horror I must have slept. I was aroused from my stupor late in the afternoon.

The noise of another terrific bombardment was the cause. I glanced behind me as the ground seemed to shake

*July 1st 1916 Alone with Death*

July 1st
1916
Purgatory

under me. Oh God what a sight I saw, I'm sure my hair stood straight. The ground seemed a mass of fire. Shells were dropping in hundreds and seemed to be leaping towards where I lay. I now gave up all hopes of life and hoped for a quick death. With my teeth tightly clenched I awaited the worst. I seemed to be almost covered with mud, my face and hands were bleeding. I suffered the tortures of the damned. Then the line of fire lifted and passed over me and was pounding on Fritz's line. I heard after they kidded him up we were going to attack here again. Instead they went over at Hebuterne on our right.

July 1st
1916
Nightfall

At last darkness slowly began to fall. But Jerry made it almost like day, by the Verey lights he sent up in hundreds. Then I saw the Germans crawling out and turning the bodies of our chaps over. I thought it time to get a move on. I wriggled backwards for a good way, dragging yards of broken wire with me that was stuck in my clothes. It ripped my flesh but I took no heed of that. I got it off me, then I got up and started to run, or rather stagger, I was so done up. As I did, other forms rose from the ground. They were 5th and 6th North who had been wounded and one or two who had been left on No Mans Land and could not get back.

Fritz saw us and turned his machine guns. What a rush for the advance trench. A chap named Jack Heywood who had been lying close to me all day tumbled in the trench along with me. We were a nice pair of broken down nervous wrecks. We simply lay on our backs in the bottom of the trench, too beat to move for a while. After we had rested for a spell we made our way to the front line helping one another over the dead bodies that lay in the trenches. Some of them lay under water, in places it was so deep I think some of the poor chaps must have been drowned when they were wounded it was so deep. At the first sentry post we came to we said, "Are you the Staffords". They said, "No. The Kings Own. Your division, what's left of 'em, have been taken out of line, you'll find them at Souastre."

Jack and I dragged our weary bodies along past heaps of dead boys in the communication trench where they had been piled ready to take out for burying. Through Foncquevillers on to Souastre, about 3 miles, we crawled rather than walked. There we found the Battalion, or what was left of them, lying in some old trenches.

The Quarter Master of C. Coy was serving some rum out. I went up to him. He said, "Hello, I heard you were killed old man." He shook hands with me and gave me a canteen of hot tea with plenty of rum in it. I drank it up and rolled in the trench close by and went to sleep. This would be about 3am in the morning of July 2nd. We were let alone until about 10am next morning. Then we were ordered to fall in for a roll call. Now I could see what I looked like. I was covered with blood and mud from head to foot, my hands and face were all over cuts and scratches. My clothes were in rags. Bullets had gone through the baggy part of my trousers and my haversack had bullet holes all over it. I said then, and I still say it - it was a miracle how I escaped with my life on that July 1st 1916. Truly my time had not yet come. The Battalion had about 150 men left. In my platoon there were about 7 of us and 5 of these had not been over. Only Jack Heywood and I returned out of the platoon that went over the top.

This is all I know of the Battle of Foncquevillers - or Gommecourt. Poor Jack Regan was killed here. Jack Heywood pulled through until the last months of the war, and then was killed. Jim Lloyd, writing to his wife afterwards, said one chap I felt right sorry for was Tommy Higgins, he looked a complete wreck. We left the old trenches and went into the village of Souastre. Here we found a draft of 500 men fresh from England to make the Battalion up again. We marched away in the afternoon and arrived at night at a village named Bailleumont. Here we stayed for that night.

Our rations consisted of bully beef and hard biscuits - and not too much of them as the transports were getting blown up. Next day, July 3rd, we started for a new section of the trenches to take over from another division who had got to go to the hell hole we had just come from. Where we took over this time was on the left of Gommecourt. We could hear and see the bombardment still going on there. The trenches were

July 1916
In fresh
trenches called the Ransart Sector, from the village Fritz held in front of us. We relieved a London Battalion. They asked us, "Where's that place where the heavy bombardments are taking place?" And we told them, "That's where we have just come from and where you are going to. That's what we are relieving you here for. That is the Somme." It didn't half put the wind up them. They said they were told they were going out for a rest! I'm afraid a lot of them had their long last rest later on - two days later they were in the thick of it.

We found these trenches fairly quiet compared to where we had left. The Germans were about 200 yards from us and a deep valley, or ravine as it was called, ran July 1916
Ransart
Sector/
Listening
Post between. As soon as I got in I clicked for listening-post duty along with Frank Harrison, who was L/Cpl, and two more men. This listening post was a long sap driven from our front trench and ending in a bay or hole right out in No-Mans-land. It was not amiss, only if you did not keep a sharp look out, Fritz would creep in the valley and drop bombs in the post. If we spotted him, we gave him a few rounds of rapid fire. I was on this post three days and four nights. We took it in turns to have a sleep for an hour in daytime as none of us slept at night. I can remember one day I stood leaning my head against the side of the trench and I must have fallen asleep; as I awoke I fell down. You want a sleep bad when you do that.

After this spell in the listening post our platoon went four more days and nights in the support line. This was a trench behind the front line about 50 yards off. We had to fetch the company's rations from the transport down to the front line. All the communication trenches were still half full of water from the heavy rains we had during May and June. It was just fine wading up to the waist in water for nearly a mile, with a big urn full of bully stew or tea strapped on your back. I'll bet they weighed a hundredweight. You had to carry your rifle and ammunition with you as well, as you were not allowed to move a yard without them. Talk of being beasts of burden. I think the British Tommy was one.

July 1916
At
Bailleulv
al

Since July 1st we had eaten no bread. About July 9th we got some, a two pound loaf between eight men. Needless to say there were no crumbs left. After this we came out of the trenches for a week, to a village called Bailleulval - but not to rest. "Oh dear no". Every night we were carrying cylinders of poison gas up to the trenches to the South Staffords. We started at dusk and did not get back until next morning at daylight. As usual we also had our rifles and equipment with us to balance the weight a bit!

After a week of enjoyment of this sort we went in the trenches for 8 more days then we came out to Bailleumont for 6 days. This was a nice little place. Here we were on carrying fatigues again. Another 9 days in the trenches and then out 6 days at a village called Berles on fatigues once

Bailleumont more. All these villages were close to the line and under
and Berles German shell fire. Berles was smashed up the most, as it
was very close to the line but the civvies still lived in all
of the buildings. There was one estaminet or pub at
Berles, where bullets used to come through the wall every
time Fritz used to open out a certain machine gun. But
they sold drinks there just the same. They had even a
penny in the slot piano here that we used to jig to. After 6
days here it was back in the trenches once more.

While in this sector of trenches I made the
acquaintance of the finest parson I ever knew. It was the
July 1916 Rev Studdert Kennedy, or Woodbine Willy as the boys
Woodbine called him. He was Chaplain to our Brigade for about 3
Willy months. He was the only Chaplain I ever saw in the
trenches. He was in them at all times day or night whether
Fritz was shelling or not. If we went over on a bombing
raid, he was always waiting to help the wounded in when
we came back. Then he was always handing packets of
Woodbines out. That was how he got his nickname. He
came round the trenches one day and started chatting to
me. He asked me if I was brought up in the Church. I told
him yes. He said have you been confirmed. I said no.
Then he asked me if I would be. Yes I said. So next time
we were at Berles he took me to a little church he had
fitted up, and prepared me, and some weeks later, I was
confirmed along with a lot more men by the Bishop of
Karthoum. I think Woodbine Willy was one of the best.

We had been in Ransart trenches up to the first Monday in August 1916. We were out for a week at Berles. Then we were told that we had got to dig an advance trench in No Mans Land to get our line nearer to Fritz. Those amongst us who had been in the advance trench digging at Foncquevillers, knew what to expect, but as I said before, after leaving there we had been made up again with 500 fresh men, and they did not know. They were about to learn. The whole Battalion filed out in No Mans Land with picks and shovels. The 6th North found the covering party, as they were holding the trenches. We got to work as soon as we could, as the quicker we could get a few feet down the safer we should be from Fritz's machine guns. After removing the grass we found that the ground was of rocky chalk. The picks and spades began to strike sparks, and so many men digging like madmen, began to make a noise. That was enough; Fritz opened out with storms of bullets cutting the grass all round us.

We lay flat on our faces in the bits of holes we had dug. I never thought I should have been so fond of kissing the earth, but we were only an inch or two down. I lay wondering what part of me would get hit first. Fritz was thinning us out - I could tell by the groans and cries of those of us who had been hit. Then those of us who were living got back to the front

August
1916
Trench
Mortar
battle

line trench. At the same time a regular bombardment opened out on both sides. I now saw the finest and the most awful sight that I've seen in my life, a battle of trench mortars. They were going up from both sides in all sizes. They were like red hot sparks darting through the air in hundreds and the noise of the explosions as they hit the ground was deafening. The very ground seemed ablaze. As I saw this I wondered how human beings could possibly live through it, they seemed to be dropping everywhere. We lost a lot of men that night. One chap I went to school with named Gilbert Bailey, who had only just come to France, was one of the killed. This was how we kept up August Bank Holiday.

August
1916
Made
Lance
Corporal

It was daylight when we got back to Berles. While in Ransart Trenches I was made Lance Corporal. We were in this sector a good bit, a week in, and a week out either at Berles, Bailleulval, or Bailleumont. Although at these places we had to go on fatigues, carrying barbed wire, trench boards or gas cylinders, and sometimes we would be marched miles away to unload trucks of timber for making trench boards, we managed to enjoy ourselves when we had the chance.

September
Concert at
Berles

At these villages we used to get concerts up among us although they were always being shelled night and day. At Berles we were having a concert in the school room, and shells were dropping all round. I remember Woodbine Willy singing 'Mother Machree' when one dropped close to. The next time we came out of the line the school was in ruins. With us it was "Eat drink and be merry today, for tomorrow you may die".

September
1916
A Near
Shave

I had one or two narrow shaves from death in these trenches. Once I was going up the communication trench to Battalion Headquarters. Old Fritz was dropping shells ahead and I would run to get past there before he dropped another. At last I heard one coming for the place I was in and I could not run another step. It hit the edge of the trench and the earth giving way, it rolled in right at my feet. I stood rooted to the spot. Then I saw that the nose cap had not come off and it would not explode. When I got out of the trench I met the Regimental Sergeant Major and he said "Hello Corporal, you look white". I said, "I feel white, Sir". Then I told him what had happened. He said, "A near shave, still a miss is as good as a mile". On September 19th I was in a dug out with some more men when a shell dropped on it and buried us. A post falling across to the side of the dug out where I lay saved me from being stiffed. When they got us out I was the only one unhurt. I got a birthday card from the wife next day. It said on it "A Happy Birthday". Happy! We'd just been buried, and were up to the hips in water as it had been raining heavy for the last week or two. I was close to Jack Thorley, who lived in Paddock Street before he enlisted, when he got his death wound. A shell dropped in amongst us and killed one man outright and poor Jack died next day.

October
1916
Saulty
A Poison
Gas
Course

On October 16th I was sent to a place called Saulty on a N.C.O.s Gas Course. I was sent straight from the trenches. I remember going to Lieut. Fielding who was our C.O. at the time for some money. He gave me 20 francs out of his own pocket and entered it in my pay book. I don't know if he got it back again as I never heard any more about it. I was at Saulty for a week on this Gas Course. There were N.C.O.s there from every battalion in the division. Saulty was Divisional Headquarters, about 8 miles from the trenches. They taught us all they knew up to then, about poison gases. There were only 3 kinds then, Chlorine and Phosgyne - these were asphyxiating gases, it was death to breathe in. The other kind was Tear Gas. This filled your eyes with water and made you blind. I went in especially prepared chambers full of the different gases. First with gas masks, smoke helmets and other kinds of respirators. Then we had to go in without them on, but with them ready, the same as we carried them about with us always. This was to test us how quick we could do it. We were quick enough I can tell you, as we knew two or three breaths of that and we only wanted burying. When I got back to the battalion they were in the trenches again.

Then I was picked out to go on a bombing raid over to Fritz. We went out to Bailleumont to practice it. When it came off it was not a success. Fritz spotted us and all we got was some killed wounded and missing; as usual I escaped again. While at Berles I found a silver crucifix in a ruined house. I carried this with me till I got home again. Soon after the raid I had a cable from the wife saying Dad was on his death bed. Could I get home to see him. I tried, and asked Woodbine Willy to help me, but it was no use they would not give me leave.

Since my pal Arthur Lomas had been killed, I was paling on with Frank Harrison. He was a L/Cpl as I was. We were like two brothers, we ate, drank and slept together and whatever we had, money or anything, we always went halves. He was a pal to me, and a good one. I often think of him. He's out in France and a small stone tells who he is. He is resting close to where he fell, doing his bit. I shall never forget him. "My Pal". "Rest In Peace." Poor Frank did not get killed until March 1917. Towards the end of October 1916 we left the Ransart trenches. We first went to Bailleumont, leaving at night. We next stayed at a village called Humbercourt for a night.

Then we started off the next day and came to a place called Lucheux. On this march I had to give up for the first time ever on the march. Just after we left Humbercourt I felt a nail sticking in my heel. I marched miles in pain then I had to ask the officer to let me fall out. I took my boot off, and found a nail sticking up in the heel about $1/2$ an inch. I knocked it down as well as I could with a stone, and a Cpl of the police helped me to hobble the remaining bit to

Lucheux. We stayed here 4 days. I remember me and Frank Harrison getting blindo here as we had just been paid out. From there we went to a place called Fortel. Jack Walker who now lives in Avery Street joined us here, it was his second time out. He had come out with us and was wounded on the Somme. From Fortel on to a village called Noyell en Chassue; here a week drilling and training. Then we marched on to a place called Domvast close to Crecy, where the English under the Black Prince defeated the French some hundreds of years ago.

All these marches were stiff ones with full kit. Still, Frank and I enjoyed ourselves out of the trenches. When we had any money between us it was vin blanc or beer, or anything we could get hold of. We stayed at Domvast about 10 days practising attacking and drilling. Then we left there and stopped at a place called Yevrounch, for 2 days. I got word that dear old Dad was dead. I wished I could have seen him before he died, but it was not to be. From here went on to a place called Rouge Fay. We were now on our way back to the trenches again. Since leaving Ransart trenches we had marched in half a circle something like this:

 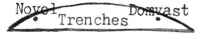

Ransant Noyel Trenches Domvast Fay Trenches

Domvast was the farthest point out.

We left Rouge Fay and came to a place called Bouque Maison. It rained in torrents all the way on this march. The water simply ran out of our boots, we were wet through. As we got close to Bouque Maison the General of the Division sat on his horse at the end of a street to watch us pass. The officers told us to look smart and cheerful as we passed him. Not an easy task when we were dead beat and soaked through with no chance of dry clothes.They served the Battalion out with box respirators here as they were a new thing. Frank was a Gas N.C.O. as well as me, and we were busy for two days taking the men in a Gas Chamber and showing them how to use the respirators. We left here and made straight for the line again. After a long march we landed dead beat at St. Amand. We stayed here one night and the next day, December 5th 1916, we took over the trenches again.

The sector we took over this time was in front of a village Fritz held named Monchy au Bois. These trenches were only about 600 yards from Bienvillers, the place we were in during the latter part of May. The old place was more smashed up now. They made it Battalion Headquarters, it was so close to the trenches. The trenches we took over were in a fearful condition. They were only about 2 foot deep in some places, and were blown to billy-o in others. To make it nice and comfortable winter was on us now, but we had got to grin and face it.

Even though Bienvillers got shelled so much now, the civvies still lived there. They seemed one and all to make a living selling coffee to the troops. I have sat for hours round a stove in the middle of the room, as there were no open fire grates in France, drinking coffee. I think it was about a penny a glass. The women used to stand at the doors and watch the shells dropping in the village, sometimes in the same street. "Ah," they would say to us, "Alemand pas bon", which means 'the Germans are no good'. It was a right place for shelling. On an average we had more men killed in Bienvillers than in the trenches. One old man lived there in a house with his daughter, and all the back room was blown away one day while they had taken refuge in the cellar. But they still wouldn't move and were still living there when I left.

After about 4 days in the trenches we were put in Bienvillers but this was as bad from the danger point of view, as houses and buildings were being blown down continually. From here we were up the trenches every night, pumping water out, digging, taking more ammunition and rations up. Sometimes when we had had a spell in the line we would go to a village about a mile beyond Bienvillers, Pommiers. This place was also under shell fire. We had to go on the same fatigues from here as we did at Bienvillers.

Then after another stay in the line we went back to St. Amand, a fairly good distance from it. Here we thought we were in clover. We were put in huts which had wooden floors and sides half way up, and canvas the other half and roof.

December
1916
St. Amand

Winter had been with us for some time now, and we knew it. The winter of 1916/17, was the worst winter I have ever known. Now you who have never left the comforts of a good fire and a warm bed just try to imagine what we went through, besides the danger of death any minute. The trenches were a morass of slimy sticky mud and water. I have stood for 4 days and nights up to the waist in muddy water. If you went in a dug out, when you were not on duty, it was generally half full of mud and water. The weather was bitter cold, as we were in open country here. We wore rubber boots with legs that came up to the thighs. A lot of these had holes in that let water in as soon as you got in it, and the water was so high in parts that they were often filled with water from the top. We were in all weathers, rain, snow, sleet and frost.

1916
Winter in
the
Trenches

The rubber boots we wore were often dragged off by the clinging mud. It would be an hours hard work to get 60 yards along the trench. Then you would be lucky if you had not lost one or both your gumboots. You put your foot down and you would feel the mud sucking you down to the thigh. It took all the strength you had got to pull your leg out to make the next step forward. Then you would stand to get your breath and while standing you were being sucked in the mud more firmer. Then it was a struggle to start off again. If you kept your gumboots on, you thought how lucky you were. I have seen men in the trenches without boots on many a time.

Winter
1916
A Sea of
Mud

The conditions were terrible. Wet all the time. Mud everywhere. In the dugouts they fair stank with the mud and water, that oozed in them. It was mud, mud everywhere, a world of mud. On your clothes, hands, and face, on the food you ate, you got it covered before you ate it. It was on your rifle and you were always cleaning it. We walked in mud, stood in it, sat in it, lay in it, and slept in it.

Ice and Snow

The cold was intense. Lots of the men suffered from frostbite, although we rubbed our feet with whale oil whenever we had the chance. I have felt at times almost like howling with pain from the cold when it was snowing. It was a terrible life. It was only the rum that they served out to us night and morning that kept our blood in circulation. When we came out of the line, we were not much better off. Our wet things had to dry on our bodies, and when we came out we were back in the night, pumping and carrying. The only difference was that we weren't holding the line. At St Amand in the huts I mentioned before, broken icicles would fall from the canvas roof on you, as you lay huddled up on the floors trying to get warm.

We were in the trenches on Christmas Day 1916. What a Christmas it was, up to the waist in water and mud and snowing heavy. Our meals that day were a 2lb loaf for five men and a tin of Machonice for the same number. How we thought of home that day - the thoughts of the

1916
Christmas
in the
Trenches

good times we had had in Christmases gone by. There was a war on now though and we in the trenches knew it. Fritz treated us to plenty of shelling and we returned the compliments for the season in the same manner.

On December 27th we came out of the trenches to St. Amand. Here they did their best to make things a bit like Xmas. They gave us some roast beef, some pudding and slab cake, some fags and plenty of French Beer. These things were dished out so much per man and we carried them to the huts, sat in groups and ate them. On December 30th we were back in the trenches once more. It was a continual grind of patrol, sentry duty and pumping water out and trench repairing. It was a fearful condition of life. Death all round you, and exposed to all weathers day and night.

While at Berles I found a silver crucifix in a ruined house.
I carried this with me till I got home again.

# 1917

On New Years Eve 1916 Fritz was shelling us like hell. Our Platoon had two men killed at 5 minutes past twelve. I remember being in charge of the party that carried the bodies out, one of them had his skull smashed and you could hear the loose bones in his head rattling as they jogged along the trench. When we first went in these trenches, they were badly battered down, and the winter storms had made them much worse. They then formed a party of men, and N.C.O.s with some Officers, from the 4 battalions of the Brigade. This was called the pioneer party. They had to repair the trenches and dig them deeper. I was picked for this party in January 1917.

We were in an old barn at Pommiers. We went to the trenches early in the morning and got back at night. The best thing about it, you had most of your nights under cover. Sometimes you had to go out at night carrying trench boards. Once on one of these journeys Jerry deluged us with gas shells. This was where my gas course helped me - I soon had my mask on and was able to help one or two that had been gassed. The deepening of the trenches turned out to be very hard work as it started to freeze, and the frost lasted about eight weeks. Then the mud and earth became as hard as rock. We had a party digging day and night turn about. When I was on nights I spent the most of my time and money drinking coffee at a French woman's house. After some time the pioneers broke up and we were sent back to our battalions. Ours were in the trenches where I rejoined them.

March
1917
No Man's
Land
Patrol

The first night in I was picked for a No Mans Land patrol to see how Jerry was going on. This was a ticklish job as it was a bright moonlight night. It was only 50 yards to Jerry's wire, and he was always dropping trench mortars in our trench and in No Man's Land. One night one of our patrols were just getting out of our barbed wire. Jerry spotted them and blew them to bits with a mortar. One of the poor chaps was Arthur Roberts of Birches Head. His mother asked me how he died when I came home again, but of course I did not tell her the full details.

March
1917
Bienvillers
and on the
March

On March 5th 1917 we were relieved by another division. We drew out and stayed at Bienvillers for the night. What a night that was. Jerry was blowing the place to bits. Houses and barns were crashing everywhere, and he was sending gas shells over in hundreds. I was picked this night to take charge of a guard. As we went through the ceremony of mounting the guard, the shrapnel was flying all over the streets. Still we had to carry on as though we were in England. The next day we started on a long march. We went through Pommiers, St. Amand, Gaudiempre, and a fairly large town called Pass. Towards evening we got to a place called Halloy after marching about 20 miles. We thought we were in for a rest. I can remember Frank Harrison wanted to bet on it, but just at this time Fritz was retiring from the Somme. So after 2 days at Halloy we were recalled to the line again.

We set off and got to Souastre, and here we stopped. Then we heard that the Germans had left Gommecourt where we attacked on July 1st the year before, and that he had gone to Bocquoy. From there we had got to attack and drive him farther on. We practiced the attack for some days in some fields close to Foncquevillers. At this same spot a few months before it was certain death to show yourself. But Fritz was a mile or two away now. At about 4pm in the afternoon of March 12th we paraded at Souastre to start for Bocquoy where we were to make the attack. I remember the song had not long been out, "If you were the only girl in the world, and I was the only boy". The lads were all singing this as we lined up. Then we were served out with barbed wire cutters, bombs and extra ammunition, and off we started, some of them never to return.

It was a long way, and we were tired when we got to Gommecourt. The night was pitch black and it was weary marching when you could hardly see anything round you. We had a shock as we left Foncquevillers and got on the Gommecourt Road. A mule and its driver taking shells up was blown up close to us by a shell from Fritz. The shells the mule was loaded with also exploded, and killed some of our men. When we got to the far outskirts of Gommecourt we halted close to what had been a wood before the war, this was now stumps of trees. It was called Biez Wood. Here we threw ourselves down to rest. It was now about midnight. The cookers had now come up, and they served us out with some warm tea; although it wasn't hot this was something to put spirit into you before going to face death. From where we lay resting, we could see Fritz sending up Verey lights. It was a good way off, but it was all open ground in front of us.

March
1917
Last talk
with my
pal

Me and Frank Harrison lay together in a hole having a last smoke before moving. We had a ground sheet over us, so that Jerry could not see the glow of our pipes. I then saw that Frank looked downhearted. I said, "Cheer up, it will soon be over". He tried to laugh it off, and he said to me "I feel as though I shall stop one this time, Tommy". I said, "Don't talk silly, Frank, we shall pull through the same as ever", but as he still looked sad I said no more.

At about 1am of the 13th March we moved from Biez Wood and after trudging along in the dark over shell holes full of water and muddy roads, we were stretched out in two long lines. The REMEs (Royal Engineers) had pegged a white tape down to show us the starting point right facing the trench where Fritz had retired to. Here we stood for about 10 minutes. Then our artillery crashed out. Off we went following the barrage of fire from our guns. The Battle of Bocquoy had begun. We followed up

March
1917
The Attack
on
Bocquoy

the curtain of fire from our guns that kept leaping on towards the German trenches. Then Fritz opened up. He put a barrage of shell fire right behind us. We were then between two fires. On we went. As I said the night was black before the attack started, now what with the thousands of shells exploding and the Verey lights going up it was as light as day. Men were falling in all directions but the living took no notice, and kept on, filled with the determination to get to the German trenches and have it out man to man. With shells and bullets he mowed our boys down in dozens. It was literally raining shrapnel. It pattered on our steel helmets as we went.

March
1917
Held by
barbed
Wire

At last after what seemed a lifetime we reached his barbed wire. Our shells had hardly touched it. Then we had to use the wire cutters under a rain of bullets and bombs. Some of us got through it, lots were killed amongst it. The trench was full of Germans who were throwing bombs and dropping mortars amongst us in the wire. We were like flies entangled in a spiders web. We put some of his machine guns out of action with bombs. We could only get into his trench one or two at a time owing to the struggle to get through the wire. Most of those who got in were killed.

March
1917
Death of
Frank
Harrison

The Germans swamped us. There were too many for us, as fast as we killed them with bombs and bayonet, others came up to take their places. I saw my mate poor Frank Harrison amongst the wire, dead. Close to him was

Capt Felix Wedgwood, he was riddled with bullets. Most of our Officers were now dead.

March
1917
Beaten
back

Then Fritz had a lot of reinforcements that rushed over the top from his rear. Things were hopeless now. We started to retire. As we retired we came across a communication trench leading to Fritz's front line. Our platoon officer named Cliff got a lot of us together, me among them, and started to go along it hoping to get Fritz on the flank. I remember we had a little Cockney among us who had the wind up bad. He said, "If that bloody fool of an Officer thinks he is going to take us back to that hell, I'll send him to hell himself with a bullet through him", and I'm sure he meant it. He seemed half crazed with fear. We had not gone far before we were up to past the knees in soft mud; we were hopelessly bogged down.

March
1917
Bogged
down in
German
Line

We could see Fritz lower down the trench sending lights up but we could not get any closer than to fire at him as we could hardly move for mud. Then daylight came. Then what a fix we were in. We could not get back over the top as we should have been wiped out before we could get to safety. At each end of the trench Fritz was there. We had to make the best of a bad job and stick it all day in the trench. Remember this was early March. I think I have never spent a colder day in my life and under such conditions. Our legs were deep in the mud and our teeth chattered from the cold. When we sat down we had to sit right in the mud. We were both hungry and tired. We were in a nice fix. The remains of the Battalion had retired about dawn, so we were left to our fate. If Fritz had come over the top to us we were at his mercy. All our rifles were clogged up with mud and try as we would we could not put them right with so much mud around us. The officer's revolver had been smashed with a piece of shrapnel and we had only about 6 bombs left between us.

The day dragged wearily on, and to make it more cheerful it started raining. I could not keep from trembling with the cold. Then Fritz dropped a few shells over us. We ate our emergency rations then we turned the dead men over who were lying all about us and shared their rations up between us. About midday Fritz sent an aeroplane over us, we could see the German's face as he looked over at us. He flew along the trench firing his machine gun into us as he went along. He went back to his own line again, and he must have taken us for dead for no more shells came over during the day. We must have looked like dead men lying in the mud, and there were dead men lying all around us.

March
1917
Out of the
Trench
At last dusk began to fall, and never was it more welcome. We started to help one another out of the trench. We could hardly walk, our legs were so cramped. As we were getting out, we saw Jerry coming over towards us. They were about 200 strong. We did not wait to shake hands with him, as we were only about 20 strong now. Off we went as fast as our cramped legs would

carry us floundering along through slush and mud. Fritz opened fire on us but his aim was uncertain in the gathering darkness and none of us were hit. At last we got to some outposts of Notts and Derbys but there were no trenches until you got to Gommecourt a good way back. The Notts and Derbys opened rapid fire on Fritz when we said he was coming over.

Reach
Foncquevillers

We dragged our weary bodies along roads swimming in water through Gommecourt up to Foncquevillers, resting now and again in old German dug outs especially when he was shelling. When we got to Foncquevillers he was shelling like hell and dropped one in a barn right by us, we were hit with pieces of timber and stones, but no one was seriously hurt. Under the ruins of the old church at Foncquevillers was an old cave hewn out of the chalk on which the church was built. We were dead beat to go any further so we crawled down there for the night. We were cold, wet, tired and hungry. We had no food to eat so we tried to sleep. The next morning we set off for Souastre. We left about seven of the men at the first aid place in Foncquevillers suffering from trench fever. The rest of us got to the Battalion at Souastre about midday. They had given us all up for dead. They gave us a dinner, the first meal since before the attack.

The Battalion had lost very heavy in Officers and men. After a day or two at Souastre we moved to a village close to the old line called Braycourt. We only stayed here one night then we heard that Fritz had retired from Bocquoy where we had attacked him.

Then we went to Gommecourt where we were put in German dugouts. I made a note in my diary at the time. "A German dugout. These are the warmest and best quarters I have been in ever since I had been out in France." His trenches were deeper, a lot better than ours. If he had been living in the mud baths we had been in all the time I think he would have given in. We found all our dead at Bocquoy. They were all buried in Biez Wood. Frank Harrison my pal, Capt Felix Wedgwood and all the other Officers, and men were all buried there. It is close to where they fell.

*March 1917 Gommecourt again*

Now I can give a description of what the village of Gommecourt looked like. It was a flattened heap of broken bricks. You could not tell where the church had stood. Of the famous Gommecourt Wood all that remained was broken stumps of trees, not a leaf grew on them. Dud shells, and holes, and torn up trees lay everywhere. On the old No Man's Land between Foncquevillers and Gommecourt, where we attacked on July 1st 1916, the bodies of the men who fell that day were lying about in hundreds. These were nothing but skeletons now. There were bodies even still lying in the barbed wire - Fritz had not disturbed them. We had to collect the equipment off them. When we moved them they fell to pieces I expect the rats had eaten at them as well as the weather rotting them away.

*What Gommecourt looked like*

The old advance trench was full of them. There were no end of grinning skulls that had rolled away from their bodies lying about. I thought at the time how strange it seemed to be walking on the place where a few months before it was raining death and destruction, as the hundreds of bodies lying about told its tale.

March
1917
Mending
roads
While here we went mending roads at Bocquoy where Fritz had mined them and blown them up. We did the same kind of work at Puisieux, Ransart and Essarts. While out on this work one day the dugout our platoon lay in got set on fire. Our packs with our kits were in it, and for weeks we hadn't got even a towel to wipe on.

After a few days we marched away from Gommecourt. We travelled along the Somme valley, and stayed at a place called Bertram Court. We stayed one night. Off again we went next day to a village named Le Condette, just one night there. Then off again to a place called Harponville. We left Harponville, and after a march of a few miles, we found a fleet of motor buses and lorries awaiting us. We got on and rode for miles. We went through the city of Amiens, a beautiful place. We went about four miles farther on, and stopped at a village called Gugium Court. We stayed here three days. Then about four o'clock one morning we marched to a railway station. We were put in cattle vans, and after a journey lasting until early the next morning we arrived at a place called Mollingham. From here we marched to a village called Borecq. We were here about a week. We had a divisional route march here. All the Battalions in the Division were on the march together, it was a miserable march. Easter passed while we were here. On Easter Tuesday we were on the march again, we passed through two big towns on the way called Arie and Lillers.

Then we came to Bethune and here we stopped.
Bethune was a nice city, but the Germans had knocked it about a bit with long range shells and airplanes. Still it was full of civvies. I saw a queue here of nearly a battalion of men all waiting for the red lamp to open at six o clock. While at Bethune, I had to prepare a tear gas chamber and put the battalion through it, to test their gas masks. I was assisted by the Medical Officer. I had to do this as I was now Gas N.C.O. I was on this job all day. In the evening I called in on an estaminet for a drink, the place was full of soldiers. I sat by the fire and noticed chaps were wiping their eyes and going out. I began to feel tears in my eyes myself, and I did not tumble to it until two or three chaps rushed to the door to see if Fritz was dropping tear shells. It was my clothes, with being in a tear gas chamber all day, they had got soaked in it. When I sat by the stove in the pub it began to evaporate in the air. I drank up and went out. They told me towards the end of the war, Bethune was nothing but a ruin.

After a week here we marched off again, and at the end of a long march, we came to a place the British called

April
1917
Arrive at
Petit Sains Petit Sains, the proper name was Sains en Gohelle. This was a colliery village and the civvies were still living there. This was our stopping place when out of the line. It was about 4 miles from the line itself. The 6th North Staffs took over first the sector we had to hold. It was close to Lens. It was called the Hulloch, Loos and Lens Sector. I think they ought to have called it Hell-fire-broke-loose sector. It would have been about right.

April
1917
The Lens
Sector          We had been told it was the hottest part of the Line, and before we had been at Petit Sains a day or two, we could well believe them. The bombardments night and day were awful. Petit Sains got shelled, now and again, but it was not enough to drive the civvies away. They even worked in the coal mines at night. We had a change from barns to sleep in here - we lay on the bare boards of bedrooms in the houses and the French people slept in the other parts of the houses downstairs. I suppose they thought if shells hit the house we should get the first benefit of it. It still seemed like heaven to lie on bedroom floors, and a good roof overhead. Petit Sains was a cheerful little place, and we enjoyed ourselves here.

May
1917
Off to the
line          After a few days we had our orders, up the line. We started at dusk. The battalion went off in small parties, about 50 yards between each party. This was on account of Fritz shelling the roads. He was shelling them around here all the time. I think we had all got the wind up pretty badly as we could guess what sort of a

place we were going to by the continual bombardments, and from what the division we relieved told us about it.

May 1917
A Windy
Journey

So on we went, shells dropping, some times just behind us missing us by inches. It was a windy journey. Then we reached a place called Angres, close to the line. As the section I was in charge of got to an old ruined house, and by now it was pitch dark, there was a sudden roar, and blinding flash. Down we went in a heap in the roadway. Then we had to laugh - it was a battery of our own guns that we could not see in the dark. They had fired just as we got close to, and the wind of the discharge had taken us off our feet. It did not steady our nerves much all the same.

May 1917
Leivin

At last we got to a town as big as Hanley. This was called Leivin. It was terribly smashed up. Pavements and tram rails torn up by shells. Shops and houses blown to ruins. Concrete dugouts had been made in the square of the town by Fritz - he had only been driven out of this place a week or two before. The town was in reality our second line trench, but there were hardly any trenches here. We were in cellars, under the ruins of the houses and shops. In the cellars were beds, chairs, pianos and all sorts of things lying about. There was no end of women's clothing and some dead women were found in one or two cellars, as though they had been gassed. Jerry seems to have done himself well in Leivin. The town was on the outskirts of Lens. It would be the beginning of May when we got here. We took over the front line next night. What a hellhole.

The line was made up of old German gun pits, shell holes and cellars under the ruins. We hardly knew where Fritz was. We went out at night looking for him. When you did find him, it was kill or be killed. Fritz was doing the same as us, hiding in deep cellars. It was at night we went about the ruins. Bullets, shells and trench mortars came from all corners, you hardly knew where they were coming from. In the daytime our platoon were in a German gun pit. He spotted us going in, and for a whole day he tried to blow us out of it. He dropped shells and mortars on top, and all round, but it was one of his own making and was too strong for him to smash up.

*May 1917*
*Holes and*
*Cellars*

He tried to get one in the entrance many a time. I was standing at the top of the stairs with another chap when he dropped one just outside. The concussion blew us right down into the gun pit. I nearly got shell shock that day. If he had have got it in, it would have blown the whole platoon to kingdom come. The trench mortars here were the biggest and the most awful I had ever seen. One of our platoons was completely buried in a cellar by the trench mortars. After a day or two of this we went back to Leivin. It was as bad here, only we were out of trench mortar range, but Fritz made up for it by shells.

*May 1917*
*A German*
*Gun Pit*

One night we were in the cellars at Leivin. It was May 5th 1917 and Fritz started sending gas shells over in thousands along with high explosive shells. He kept this up for about 12 hours. I had a nice time of it now. As I

May
1917
Gas
Shells

was Coy Gas N.C.O. I had to go out in the storms of shells, and visit the cellars where the men were taking precautions with their gas masks and blankets soaked in chemical preparation, hung over holes in the cellars. I went out with my mask on, and in the streets the gas hung in the air like a fog. I had to grope my way about the smashed up streets, as I could hardly see with my mask on, as it was night and the eye holes kept getting dimmed up. There was not a soul about that ruined town, everybody was in dugouts and cellars away from the shells that were dropping everywhere. I expected to get killed any minute, if not with shells, by the houses and walls, that were falling all over the place. I was just missing death by inches as I went stumbling about.

I had to obtain a report of every Officer in charge of men, and then report to headquarters. The cellars took some finding in the dark, and the fog of gas about. I had a stick that I found in a cellar the day before, this helped me about same as a blind man. I've got that stick yet, it is at home with the name Leivin carved upon it. A friend brought it back for me when he came over on leave. It was a night I did not expect to see daylight, but duty had to be done, and I got through with a few bruises from stumbling down and flying stones. There was over 200 men gassed that night, a lot of them died as it was a deadly gas, named Phosgene. Two breaths of it was fatal.

May
1917
A Nice
Job

The next night, May 6th, we went to the outposts

again, that represented the firing line. I had to stop at Coy headquarters in case of more gassing. Then I should have had to go round with the Company Officer. Headquarters consisted of a cellar that had once had a house over the top of it, but the house had been blown away by shells and the cellar was simply a hole in the ground. He did not gas us, but he trench mortared and shelled us like hell. I was alone with the Company Officer in that cellar.

During the night, we could hear the shells thudding and exploding in the ground all round us. If one of the mortars had dropped on top, we should have been buried. I went out two or three times in the night, and the air was full of flying shrapnel and it seemed to be raining fire. It seemed an eternity to us two, under such a bombardment, in that old cellar. If a shell happened to drop close to the opening, the fumes almost choked us. The Officer said, "I think we are in a nice grave for two." We had both got the wind up a bit. Towards daybreak the Sergeant Major crawled in. He said our losses were awful. Fritz slackened off at daylight. The next night it was as bad again but the old cellar still stood.

About May 13th we went back to Petit Sains, and we were not sorry, we were all nerves and our losses were terrible. We were glad to get back to civilization again. It was like leaving hell and going to heaven. It was worth something to get a decent sleep again, even if it was only on bare boards. We had not had much time to sleep in the hellhole we had just left. After about six days we went up the line again. I remember the evening we started up, we had a church service, it was a Sunday. The service was held in an open square. At the end of it, we finished up by singing, 'God Save the King'. It seemed alright, men who had got to face death in terrible forms, singing God save a man, who was safe and in comfort, away from shot and shell, in England.

We went this time on the left section. It was called the Loos sector. It was the same here as at Leivin, ruins and cellars, but there were a lot of old trenches here, dug through the ruins. They had some sinister names attached to them as well, such as Hell Fire Corner, Coffin Trench and Bloody Lane. It told you what sort of a place it was. Here we were shelled and gassed almost all of the time. We did the longest spell in the line I had ever done. It was 28 days. We were days at a time, not even daring to slip our boots off to ease our feet. Many a time we should be over two days without a wink of sleep. When we did sleep it was only for an hour or two at a time. It was such a hot show. Fritz was always doing something to keep us at it. He was either coming over on a raid, or shelling us, or gassing us. I could have slept walking about.

On the 28th day in the line, we were told we had to make a raid on Fritz. Our Coy, which was C, and A Coy, were to do it.  The two Companys were taken out of the line for two days to practice the raid.  We were taken to a village close to named Bully Greenay.  The day we went back up the line again, we were paid out.  My pay book is signed by an officer named Cliff, he was killed in the stunt.  He was with us at Bocquoy.  I think we all had a drunk up with our money - we never knew, it might be the last some of us would have the chance of spending it.  We got up the line, and stayed in cellars till about 6pm on June 14$^{th}$.  We came out of our holes, and got in the old trenches ready.  Then our artillery barrage opened up.  They sent liquid fire shells over in hundreds.  It was a grand and terrible sight.  The earth seemed to be on fire.  Then we saw a lot of Germans who had been in listening posts rushing towards their lines, with flames all around them.  They did not get far, we riddled them, as they were getting through their wire, where they hung like scarecrows.  But we did not have it all our own way.  Fritz was sending storms of bullets and shells among us.  Mr Cliff was fatally wounded before we had gone ten yards, and our men were being killed in all directions.

Still it did not stop us.  Our Coy got in his trenches, but A Coy were beaten back and almost wiped out.  We were in his line about 2 hours, and by that time there were only dead, and dying Germans in the part we were in.  Those who had dashed down dugouts were killed by bombs, and those who were in the trench, by bullet and

June 1917
"Mercy
Kamerad"

bayonet. The poor devils were crying "Kamerad! Kamerad!" But all the mercy they got was a bayonet stuck in the throat or body. Such is war. There is nothing nice or glorious about it, only death and destruction and sorrow for women and children. At last Fritz's artillery began to shell us in his trenches. It began to get too hot for us. We made a dash back for our line again carrying our wounded with us.

June 1917
A Narrow
Escape

We lost more men getting back than going over. It was hell itself. Shells, mortars and bullets were falling like rain. I was nearly killed just as I jumped in our trench. A big trench mortar dropped close to me, it lifted me off my feet and blew me some yards away. I was almost stunned by the noise of the explosion, and I could not see for a while. I felt as though I had been kicked all over, but except for a shaking I was unhurt, it is what is called a close shave.

We got back to the old cellars, and the next night we were taken out of the line to Petit Sains. How glad we were to see the French people where we slept, it seemed years since we saw them. As for me, it was the last time I was at Petit Sains, as I was taken prisoner the next time up the line. We were paid out on June 17th. This is the last payment entered into my pay book, it is signed by Lieut. Green, and he was killed in the next attack we were in. Most of the Officers who signed my pay book are among the killed. We were at Petit Sains 6 days. They flew all too quickly. I was sweating on coming home on leave. My wife sent a letter while I was here asking when I should come home. I sent word that I did not know, as something seemed to tell me, I should not get home for a good while. I felt that something was going to happen to me, yet all the time I seemed to know I should not be killed.

Before we went up the line we were made up to full strength again. Then we went up the Leivin sector in front of Lens. The first place we stopped in was Angres close to Leivin, and we were here for two days. The suburbs of Lens were like the Potteries, they were all grouped close to one another. At Angres there was an old castle, with a fine moat all the way round it. Here

we were bathing with shells dropping all around us. Then we moved up to Leivin, where we stayed for 2 days. We were engaged on taking up loads of bombs and ammunition to the line in front of Lens. We guessed there was something coming off.

In the daytime when we could get a bit of sleep. I passed part of my time away exploring the houses all about Leivin. It seemed pitiful to see the broken furniture lying in the houses. Treasured things like photographs still hanging on the walls. I generally went on these rambles by myself. I used to stand in the quiet and deserted houses and wonder what had happened to the originals of the photos lying about. It seemed saddening to stand there among thousands of houses, and

June
1917
A look
round the
ruins of
Leivin

no sign of life, with the crashing of big shells falling everywhere at the same time, to remind you that death was very near. It was a fairly large town, there were two or three big collieries there. It was very dangerous to go round them as they were a mark for his big guns, but I went round one. It was a sight, the head gears were smashed up, and the winding engines were wrecked. It looked as though Fritz had smashed them up on purpose. It looked as though work had ceased suddenly and everyone had fled. The Locos still stood there, with the wagons attached to them, but they were battered and torn by big shells. It only showed you how destructive war is.

On the morning of June 30th we were told we were going to make an attack on the town of Lens. We were to take up our positions that night. In the afternoon I went picking strawberries in the gardens of some houses, the shells were dropping in the gardens but it did not stop us from picking. We knew we had got to face hell again so we did not care what happened.

We moved off the same night. We lost nearly all B. Coy before we got to the starting point. They were caught in some very heavy shell fire. The jumping off place was a few trenches across main roads. These the 6th North Staffs had taken from the Germans the night before. There were no end of 6th North dead lying about as the result of the attack. Old Fritz had got the wind up pretty badly, he treated us to bullets, shelling, and thousands of coloured lights, these were signals to his artillery.

We crept out and lay down in lines among shell holes, and ruins, and waited for day to break. Fritz had seen us, he shelled and machine gunned like hell. Our Officer, W. Green was killed at the first discharge. We knew we were in for a hot time of it, by the signal lights he kept sending up for artillery fire. This was the hardest part to lie there, doing nothing waiting for the dawn, and chaps getting killed all the time. We should have all been wiped out, only the shell holes and ruined buildings protected us a bit. There we lay waiting wondering what fate was in store for us. Day was now slowly breaking, the sky was getting streaked with grey. It was July 1st, Sunday morning twelve months since our attack on Gommecourt. Was this going to be another slaughter like that? We had to hope for the best, and trust to luck.

July 1st
1917
Waiting
for the
dawn

At last our suspense was over, our artillery opened out with a creeping barrage of shell fire. We gathered ourselves up and followed it. We rushed on yelling like fiends. We could see Germans in all directions running away down streets, rushing out of houses, anywhere to get away from us, and the awful shell fire that was pounding all round them. After them we went longing to kill. At times like these man is not human. He is changed into a bloodthirsty beast. His one desire is to kill. The Germans were mowing our men down by shells and bullets. A man's brains were scattered over the left side of my face,

July 1st
1917
Attack on
Lens

and shoulder, but I did not notice it until the charge was over. Whenever a German came our way he was shot or bayoneted, there was no mercy. All we knew was that the Germans were running, and we wanted to kill as many as we could. They were the cause of the war we were told and we wanted our revenge. That is war, there we were killing human beings who had never done us any harm, whose only crime was that they were Germans. This is the result of money, kings and politics. At last we got as far into Lens as we could.

July 1st
1917
In Lens

It was now broad daylight. What a sight of blood and carnage lay around us. British and German lying around dead and dying in heaps. It was the price we paid for war. Then we saw a lot of men coming down a street towards us. At first we took them for Notts and Derbys who had attacked on the left of us. We shouted to them and they started to run back. Then we saw they were Germans, after them we went, and not one escaped, except two that we took prisoner.

After this we sent scouts out to look round how we were fixed. I was one of them. We found we were in a trap, we had got right in Lens. The Notts and Derbys were cut off from us with streets full of Germans between. We took up three rows of houses facing a big square. In one of them we captured a Jerry who could talk English, he said in the streets we had dashed through there were two battalions of Jerrys hidden in the

Our
Position cellars, these were to be reinforced by others working through the houses all around, then they were going to counter attack about midday. If another British battalion had followed us over, we should have got back, at least some of us would, but none came. Some of our planes flew over to see where we were. We lit red ground flares to show them. We waited with renewed hope then, thinking help would come, but none came. This was one of the blunders of the war. If the British had sent another Division up, we should have taken Lens that day with small loss. When the Canadians captured it about two months after they lost thousands of men.

Our case was hopeless now, all we could do was to shoot at every Jerry we could see. Fritz was dashing across open spaces and down streets in fact he was everywhere. If we saw one we shot him. If he saw us first he shot us, bullets were coming from all unexpected corners, he was at upstairs windows, all over the place picking our men off with rifle, and machine gun. I felt the wind of bullets pass me many a time. One narrow escape I had was when I had been to a house where our officer was. I had been to tell him the Germans were massing all round us, and I was just coming out of the doorway when bullets whizzed each side of my head right into the house.

July 1st
1917
Surrounded

At last he had got the houses we were in completely surrounded. He rushed at first on the front of us, but we

The
Germans
Counter
Attack

gave him rapid fire and emptying Lewis Guns into him. They fell like corn before a reaper, but more took their places. They came up the street and threw bombs in the houses. Then we started to get out of them, through windows, doors anyhow, or we should have been killed like rats in a trap. We were not much better off in the open. Fritz was firing into us on all sides and kept getting closer. We were doing our best to keep him off, but his numbers were increasing and ours were getting less. It was all up with us. Some of our lads threw their rifles down, and put their hands up to surrender. It was the signal for them to rush in on all sides to finish us off. Those who had thrown their rifles down were bayoneted without mercy. Then we became a struggling crowd of British and German. Nothing was used now, only the

Fighting
for Life

bayonet, on both sides. It was a duel to the death. Our breath was coming in gasps as we glared at one another. It was thrust and stab. We were fighting with the madness of despair. In those awful moments with death staring us in the face, how sweet life seemed. We did want to live, and we kept on killing to hold on to our own lives as long as we could. It was indeed a fight for life. A big German rushed at me. I could not stop him because a Jerry I had struck had snatched my rifle out of my grasp as he fell. I bent down and just missed the point of his bayonet, and then I saw stars. I got a clout on the head with his butt. My tin hat saved me, or it would have knocked my brains out.

July 1st
1917
Prisoner
of War

There was only about three of us left out of the group I had been fighting in. A German Officer then shouted in English, "Surrender", so we threw our rifles down, and put up our hands. Then I was taken Prisoner of War. This was the end of my last fight in the Great War. This happened on Sunday July 1st 1917. I along with the others they had captured. It would only be about fifty altogether. That was all that was left of us. We were marched through the city of Lens. There were thousands of German soldiers all around us. We had to march with our hands held up in the air. I did not think we should get through alive even then. The Germans were cuffing, and kicking us along the way. Some rushed at us with their bayonets - it was the German Officers who stopped them - and I noticed those who seemed most bitter had not been in the scrap with us.

July 1917
Searched
and
Robbed

The officers could not stop all the violence. Some of our lads got jabbed in the arms and legs by bayonets. They took everything off us they could find. It was now I lost my diary. All they left me was a photo of my wife and child, my father's funeral card and my tobacco box. I had to beg and pray as well as I could to make them understand me. I managed to keep the crucifix they missed in their search. It was one I found at Berles.

We were taken to a village just at the back of Lens. There were French people here, but I only saw women, I saw no Frenchmen. The women crowded round us saying,

"Bon Anglais", and looked pitying at us, but they fled in all directions as a German General came up. He said in English. "Good evening boys", but we did not answer him. I was getting hungry now. Then we saw them dishing food out to our guards. This seemed to make us more hungry still. We had not had anything to eat since leaving Leivin the night before. We made signs to the Germans about us, but all we got was a bucket of water to drink. Still we were very thirsty, and were thankful for that, but after quenching our thirst we felt our hunger more.

As darkness began to fall we were put in motor vans and driven further behind the line. One of the guards gave me a cigarette, and lit it for me on the way. I thought it a kind action, and felt grateful as I was longing for a smoke. After a short journey we pulled up at a big town that I found out was named Douai. It was now night. We were taken to a big barracks in the centre of the town where we had another search for documents of any kind. Then an officer who spoke in English questioned us about what regiment, what brigade, and what division we belonged to. He also asked us what we thought about the war. Did England expect to win? Were we getting short of men? He also said that the German submarines would starve England out in another month or two, and we should be glad to have peace at any price. He told us Germany was bound to win in the end. We let him have his say, we were fed up with war at any rate. Then we were taken to where we got to stay for some weeks. We had to lie on the hard floors just as we were captured, no straw, or blankets, not even a stone for a pillow. These were our conditions all the time we were at Douai.

German food

We were kept fastened up for two days in this room, and they kept asking us questions about our army, and other things. On the Monday morning July 2nd we had our first meal as prisoners. We were given a piece of black bread, and a drink of what they called coffee. The bread was made of rye and potatoes and tasted dreadfully sour. It was mouldy as well. I was hungry. I had not tasted food from Saturday night, but I could not face it. Afterwards when you got used to it the bread did not appease the hunger, you never had enough. The coffee was made of acorns roasted, and ground up, and this was served up without sugar so it tasted beautiful, I don't think! Later on when hunger grew worse we did not think of taste. I thought I had been hungry many a time, but I did not really know what real hunger was until I was taken Prisoner of War.

I had a card given to me on July 2nd to send home to say I was a prisoner. The wife did not get this until three or four months afterwards. The Germans did not send it off until I was in Germany. The reason I believe for this was that we were kept working under British shell fire, and lots of prisoners were killed. No one knew whether you had been a prisoner, or not. You were posted

In Confinement — as missing until the end of the war. The first day of captivity dragged along until midday, then there another glorious meal the Germans called mittagessen, mid-day meal. We were served out with old British mess tins. I suppose he had got these off dead men on No Mans Land. They were thick with rust, when we cleaned them with dirt there was no tin left on them, they were like old iron. These were then half filled with horse beans, and the hot water they were boiled in. The beans were almost raw, and the water had nothing in it to thicken it, so you couldn't make a mistake and call it soup. It was as clear as when it came from the tap. We were hungry now, so we did our best to nibble the beans. We found out after, this was considered one of the best meals prisoners got. This was served out again at six in the evening. On other days we had boiled up turnips or mangle-wurzels, those they fed cows on in England. The Germans thought they were good enough for prisoners to feed on. Another fearful meal was white cabbage kept until it was sour, then boiled. This was what they called sauerkraut. We only had one thin piece of black bread each morning along with the imitation coffee. Flesh meat, or fats, such as dripping or margarine, we never saw. It was always vegetables and water, which the Germans had the cheek to call soup. This is the food we had to work on behind the lines, under our own shell fire.

Hunger — We were out all day digging and laying railroads. Then we had to work on the river unloading great barges

Working
under
Shell Fire
of flint stones, as we got weaker from want of proper food, the German sentries would kick and punch us, and club us with their rifles to make us work faster. It made me think of the slaves I had read about in 'Uncle Tom's Cabin'. Still I think the slaves were better fed than us, as a slave costs money, and it did not matter whether we lived or died, there were plenty of prisoners and they cost nothing.

French
People at
Douai
Their
kindness
to us
As we went to our toil through the streets of Douai, the French who lived in that city, would raise their hats as we passed along. It was a mark of respect for poor unfortunate British Tommys. When the Germans took our steel helmets off us, after we were taken, we had to go bare headed, but the French people came running out of shops, and houses, and threw us hats, and caps of all kinds, even taking them off their own heads. I had a brand new trilby given me, and I wore it for months, until I got a uniform cap from England. When the sentry was not looking they gave us pieces of bread, which were eagerly devoured. Also now and again we would have fags given us, these were almost as welcome as food as we could not get a smoke for weeks at times.

The poor civvies often went through the mill for trying to be kind to us. I have seen many a man and woman knocked over by the sentries' rifles for it. I began to know what starving was now. We never got enough to eat even of the rubbish they gave us. It was just enough to keep life in us, and some of the poor chaps died as it was. It was terrible, the continual gnawing pangs of hunger, you dropped off to sleep at night craving for a good meal and awoke hungry just the same. The rubbish they gave you for meals, only tantalized your hunger the more. I know for six months I never had a satisfying meal. There was a big lot of prisoners at Douai. They were from every regiment in the British Army. We were herded together like a lot of pigs. We lay on the floors just as we were captured. We did not undress, as we had only the bare floor to lie on, and had nothing to cover us with.

Hungry, and Verminous

We got in an absolutely, filthy, verminous condition. We had no soap to wash ourselves with. The Germans had no soap for themselves, only substitute soap, but we did not get that even. I did not shave for weeks, and when I did, it was only with a jack knife I sharpened up. I was lousy many a time when in the trenches, but we did get a bath now and again, and clean clothes then. Here there were no baths, soap or clothes. I wore the same shirt for months. We were that crumby, lice walked all over us, and on the floors we lay on. What a life. Worn out weak and ill for want of food, dirty and verminous. We were driven out day after day, to all sorts of hard labour helped along

Worse than slaves

with insults and blows from the sentries. Then a chance of getting killed by British shells. This was our condition as Prisoners of War at Douai. At last I got so weak and ill from starvation and ill treatment, I could hardly get along.

August
1917
Leaving
Douai
Then I was picked out with about fifty more men in the same condition, to go to Germany. It would be about the last day of August. We were given a double ration of bread, and were told it had got to last until the end of our journey. It was on a Friday afternoon, we marched down to the station with sentries each side of us. We got in cattle vans along with the sentries and off we started for Germany. I shall never forget that journey as long as I live. The bread they had given us to last was eaten before Friday night. Then I was as hungry as I was before. I could have eaten ten times as much, and then not be satisfied, but there was no more to eat, so I had to hitch my belt up another hole, and look happy. When the sentries in the van ate their meals, it was torture to us to watch them. We felt like snatching it out of their hands, but we dare not. They were armed and we were helpless.

Through
Belgium
A
Hungry
Journey
We went through Belgium, through Valcenes, through Louvain that they burnt in 1914. We stopped at the station in Brussels. Here a Belgian got stabbed in the arm by a bayonet, for trying to give us some bread. We left here at daylight on the Saturday morning. I should have enjoyed the passing scenery better, if I had not have been so hungry. The sentries had the van doors open by day, so we could see the country, as we went along. We passed orchards hung with fruit ready for plucking. Oh how we longed to get in them, but it was like the fox and the grapes, it was all sour for us.

Arrive in Germany    We got to Aix le Chappelle late on Saturday night, and stayed in the station some hours. Here we crossed the border of Belgium into Germany. Then on through Cologne and Essen on to Dusseldorf. It would be midday Sunday now. We stopped here about an hour. Then one of the guards let me get out on the platform to pick cigar and cigarette ends up, for myself and mates. I filled my pockets and we had the first smoke for days. The German people on the stations we stopped at crowded round to stare at us, but we did not mind we were used to anything now. The next stop was at a place called Wanne. Here the German officer in charge, who seemed a decent chap, managed to get us a bowl of soup from a German soldier's mess room. We were very thankful for it as we had not tasted any food since the Friday. When we gave the officer thanks, he was very pleased. All the same, I should have liked something solid to get my teeth into.

Arrive at Dulmen    On the Sunday evening we got to a place called Haltern. Here we got off the train stiff with the long ride. I could hardly walk I was so stiff, but we had to march about 4 miles, to a place called Dulmen. Here there was a huge Prisoners Camp. Dulmen was in Westphalia. We were put in a big hut with no bedding, and earth floor to lie on for the night. We were then given a bowl of barely gruel, and locked in. Next morning, we had a thin slice of black bread and the usual coffee. After this we were taken to another big hut and ordered to strip. Our clothes were then fumigated to kill the livestock in them. Then they cut our hair as close to the head as possible, and shaved the hair off our bodies. We then had a shower bath, plenty of hot water but no soap. Then we got our clothes back very much worse for wear, and were put in a big isolation hut. We were kept in here about a week. During this time we were inoculated about five times, also vaccinated. Then we went in the main camp. Here the fleas were in the huts in thousands, you could not sleep for bites. We were allowed to write home from here, but you had to buy your own paper to write on. A mate gave me some. We were told it would be 8 or 10 weeks before we got any letters, or parcels of food from England. If we were moved before that length of time, it would take longer.

We were now taken out every day on working parties, to work for the miserable starvation diet we got. The food here was worse if anything than at Douai. I got thinner every day, my clothes simply hung on me. Some days it was impossible to tell what the soup they gave us was made of. At times it was just like dirty water with sand at the bottom. One day when our so called soup was boiling in the coppers, there came in the camp about five thousand British, French and Belgian Prisoners. To make the soup go round, the Germans simply put more water in, to make more of it.

At meal times you could see us scrounging all round the camp, with our bowls, after leavings of soup

Ever
Hungry

off the French and English prisoners who were getting parcels through. There were thousands of Russian prisoners in the camp. They got nothing from Russia. They had to go on the scrounging way, the same as us. There was many a fight between us, as to who should get the leavings. But as much as we got, it did not fill you it only bloated you up with water. When you got your daily piece of bread, you had to eat it at once, or it would get stolen off you by your hungry mates. You would steal food off your best friend. Hunger knew no law. It was everyone for himself. This incident will show you how low I was brought myself. I was going round the camp

Scrounging
for Food

one day, on the scrounge as usual, when I saw a crust of black bread lying in the dirt. How long it had been there, God knows. I picked it up and ate it, dirt and all. The old proverb, "a hungry dog will eat dirty pudding" was true in my case.

Leaving
Dulmen

About the end of September, we were told we were going somewhere else. We said goodbye to parcels for a bit longer, as they had not yet come through from England. On Saturday September 27th about 100 British were given a slice of bread, our usual rations, and marched to Dulmen station, about 4 miles off. We got on a train at 6am and off we started. We travelled on through Munster and Osnabruck, on to Bremen, here we stood on the platform in the early hours of Sunday morning, shivering from cold, for three hours waiting for a train to take us to our destination. At last we were off again and arrived at Soltau in Hanover, at about 8 o'clock.

We then had a walk of about 3 miles to the prison camp. Here we were put in an isolation compound, away from the main camp. We had to wait until midday for something to eat. The bowls and spoon we had been served out at Dulmen, we carried with us. We had also what they called two blankets, mine were like two table cloths, they were so thin, but we got no more, winter or summer. They gave us a bowl of cabbage soup. It was the first food since the Saturday morning. I felt like eating bowl and spoon and all, I was that famished, but there was no such thing as second helpings. The next day we had another bath without soap, and a haircut, and a shave again. We were kept in isolation for about 4 or 5 days, doing nothing, only waiting for meal times, and when these came round, we did not get much satisfaction out of them, the same food as at Dulmen.

Arrive at Soltau

Then we were told we were to be sent out on a labour Kommando. "Ha-ha", we thought, "perhaps we shall get better food than in the prison camps". But we were soon to find our mistake out later. On Friday October 4th, off we started, the same 100 men. They were from all regiments, besides Canadians and Australians, Scotch, and Irish. About 3am, with the usual slice of bread, off we started for the station.

October
1917
Leave
Soltau

A
Mountain
Journey

We got on the train, and another hungry journey commenced. We went through Hildeshiem, Madgeburg, Halberstadt, on to Blankenburge. This was the start of the Harz mountain district. Here we changed to a mountain railway. Then we had a journey, climbing the side of mountains and going down into deep valleys. It was night now and you could not see outside, it was a strange experience, that switch back ride in the darkness. At last near the top of one of the highest ascents, we stopped. This we found out, was the end of the journey.

Arrive at
Elbingerode

The village was named Elbingerode. It was right among the Harz mountains. It was now about 4am on the Saturday morning. What struck us as we left the station was the extreme cold, and biting winds that blew all around us. But we would get to feel a lot colder before we left there. We were taken to what seemed to have been the village concert room at one time. There was scenery and a stage in it. There had been wooden bunks built all round the sides of the room for us to sleep in. We were ravenously hungry when we got in, so the first thing we asked for was food. They gave us a bowl of turnips cut in bits and the water for gravy. Then they let us get down in the bunks for a few hours, and as we were dead beat we forgot our troubles in sleep. About 8am we were aroused from our sleep by the sentries who had charge of us. They gave us some bread and substitute coffee for breakfast. Then we were told what we had got to do, and what we were there for.

Our Work at Elbingerode    Around the Harz mountains it was all iron mines, cement works and stone quarries. We had got to work in a stone quarry among the mountains, from 6am until 6pm. If any man refused to work, he would be made to by force. If we left the spot where we were working, without permission, you would be shot, as intending to escape. If any man struck a sentry, who was in charge of us, the punishment was death. If the sentries thought you were not working hard enough, they were allowed to club you with their rifles, and if you struck back they could shoot you. For all this you got paid 85 pfennig or 8½d a day. All this was told to us in English, by an interpreter, so that there could not be any mistake as to what we could expect.

October 1917 Start to Work    On the Saturday after midday they took us out to work. There was no Saturday afternoon off in Germany, the same as in England. At this place, we even had to work on Sundays until dinner time. When we got to the quarry, we saw what we had dropped in for. The Germans drilled and blew the rock, and we had to break it up with sledge and pick, and then load it up in iron tipping wagons. When the wagon was loaded, we had to push it to an engine, up a steep bank, which took them to a stone crushing plant. We had to take back the empties the engine had brought, to load them up. This was the process all day long. There were three or four men to a wagon, which held about 30 cwt. It was woe betide us if the wagons were not loaded by the time the engine was back from taking the last load. It was a job for a strong healthy man, and weak as we were from starvation it was torture to us.

The
Sergeant
Major

The food here was terrible, worse than any we had at the camps. There was a German Sergeant Major in charge of us. We found out that he was selling the bread, and potatoes, and anything worth eating to the villagers, instead of feeding us. The rations for us were sent from the nearest prison camp. There was none too much of them as it was, but by the time the Sergeant Major had done with them they were less. The civvies were rationed same as people in England, and were only glad to get more, and starve the "Sweinhund Englanders", as they called us. At four o'clock in the mornings we were aroused from our fitful sleep. If we did not hear the Sergeant Major shout, and tumble out of it quick enough for him, he would come round and bash you with a thick stick.

Then we should have a drink of coffee, so misnamed. The best you could say for it was that it was hot. No sugar, or saccharine to sweeten it, we hadn't any, so we put salt in it, to taste it a bit. Then we were marched off in line to the quarry, about half an hour's walk. We worked until 9am. Then we stopped for 10 minutes for another drink of substitute coffee. Then on again until 12am. Then they brought the soup up from the billet. It came on a cart in a huge tub. Oh why should they have called it soup? It ought to have been pig wash. It was various kinds. Sour cabbage

October
1917
The food
is awful

mostly, that gave us diarrhoea. At other times it would be mangel-wurzels, turnips, and at times you could not tell what it was. The only thing you were sure of was that it was mostly water. Then when we got back at night, another soup, and a slice of bread. That was the food we had to work on in a stone quarry, in all weathers.

Starvation
and cold

The cold began to be intense. It was snowing about a week after we got here, and it snowed or rained almost every day. I have never experienced such intense cold as I felt here, the biting winds that blew round the mountains went through you. Our clothes were in rags, we had only what we were captured in. My shoes were completely worn off my feet. They gave me a pair of wooden sabots to wear, they were awful to walk in, the wooden sides rubbed my feet raw. I had to wrap my feet in old rags. When I had nothing else, I ripped part of my shirt off to wrap round them.

November
1917
Weak and
ill

The men began to give in one by one. They were dropping at work like dead men. When a man fell, the sentries put them to lie in the snow until they were driven back to work again. The watery food told on us now. I was so swelled up with water my legs were all one thickness. I could hardly crawl, but I was made to work as well as I could. When I awakened in the morning, I could hardly see out of my eyes, my face was that swollen up. We looked at one another and said if the folks at home saw us now, they would not know us.

Every night we had to carry some poor chaps back to the billet, who were done for, when we could hardly drag ourselves.

When we got in we were lined up and the sentries reported to the Sergeant Major any man who they thought had not done enough work during the day. Then they went through it, that man was a devil. He spit in their faces, kicked them, and thrashed them round the room, with a club until they dropped senseless. We had to look on weak and helpless, held at bay with loaded rifles. It was horrible.

One day it was pouring with rain when we turned out. It kept on, and it was teeming off us. We threw our tools down and refused to do any more. The sentries kicked punched and threatened to shoot, but we stuck it out and they took us back to billet. That devil of a Sergeant Major met us at the doors, and he said "The Englanders want a holiday, do they?" - for by now most of us understood German. He said get inside and dry yourselves. We got in and got our tunics and shirts off and were in our bare feet getting dry as well as we could, when that devil, and the sentries rushed in the room with revolvers and rifles pointed at us. "Fall in line." he roared, "Just as you are", at the same time helping us along with kicks. "Now march", he yelled. The doors were opened, it was still pouring with rain, but we were driven out in it, as we were, and had to stand in line for about an hour. I had bare feet, but I had my shirt on. Some had their shirts

German
Brutality

November
1917
We get a
Holiday

off. The sentry stood under cover with loaded rifles pointed at us, and the Major stood grinning and asking us how we liked our holiday. The cold was terrible. After this we got no bread that day.

November
1917
Work and
Starvation

A feed of
potato
peelings

Men were dying now, we were sadly reduced in number. It was awful. It was nothing but hard work, starvation and brutality. All this time I had not received a letter or a parcel from England. I was ravenously hungry. I had struggled with the Russian prisoners who worked with us for the potato peelings that the Germans threw away. I had boiled them and eaten them with relish, and my poor mates did the same. Our wages ran to 4 marks a week. The only thing it was possible to buy were onions and apples. There was no chance of buying any other food to eat. We got 4 onions for a mark, and 2 apples for a mark, I used to buy whichever I could get and roast them. I thought roasted onions grand.

Sundays did not bring us any respite - we had to work until 1pm then we had the rest of the day off, but we only got coffee instead of soup and a piece of bread as we were not working. I was longing for a smoke and I smoked dried leaves or anything I could smoke. Men were dying off quick now, but it did not make things any better for us that were left. They said if we all died they could get more prisoners. That was all they thought about us. Slaves were treated better than us, we were no value at all.

November
1917
First
Postcard
from
home
About the end of November 1917 I got my first postcard from the wife, saying that she had paid 5s 8d for a parcel of food to the prisoners of war fund. This was the first line I had had from home since June. I had sent letters every month, but I could not tell them at home, the conditions I was in, as the letters were censored. All I dare say was I am going on well and send a parcel as soon as you can. How I read, and reread that postcard. I kissed it many a time, thinking of the one who wrote it and still cared for me. It was grand to know that someone thought of me still, among the brutal conditions I was living under. I knew that postcard off by heart. It inspired me with the will to live and get through. Before it came to me with its message of hope I wanted to die. I had thought of suicide but I could not steel myself to take my own life. Self murder takes a bit of doing. I got my

razor out that I had managed to buy. I have got the same razor at home now. I put it in my bunk many a night intending to kill myself before morning. Then I should think of home, and my wife and child, and I had not got the nerve to do it. The feeling was awful. I wanted to die and daren't. Then I would say to myself, I shall die in any case as I was getting weaker and weaker every day. It was slow labour we did now, even curses, kicks and blows ceased to put energy into us, we were past caring what happened. That postcard was a ray of hope in the darkness of despair.

The Prisoner of War Fund sent four parcels of tinned food and biscuits a month, and four parcels of bread came from Copenhagen in Denmark, which was a neutral country during the war. The reason I had not had them was with moving right across the country. At every place I had been, they were held up a week or two, before being repacked, and sent on. If you could stay long enough in one place you got the food parcels regular, and could live on them, and leave the pig wash the Germans gave you alone. About a fortnight after getting the postcard I got two parcels at once. One was a bread parcel, the other had tinned food, biscuits and Quaker oats in it. They had been on the road for months. They had been to Dulmen, Saltau, and another camp, on to Halberstadt, then to Elbingerode. The bread parcels were useless, absolutely green. It was a sight to see me picking the bread to bits to see if there was a bit in it I could eat. The Germans did what they called censoring the parcels. They opened everything that was in them. They emptied out the tea, sugar, and Quaker oats, cut the piece of soap in two, and any tins of food they kept back and gave you tickets for them. To get the tins you had to take your eating bowl. Then they opened the tins, and put the contents in the bowl. All this was done so that you could not have any secret plans or correspondence from home to aid you to escape.

The first parcel I got I nearly killed myself with

eating. The biscuits and Quaker oats soon went. There was a tin of dripping in it. As I said before I had not tasted fat food since being prisoner, and the bitter cold weather made you long for it. So I could not leave the dripping alone, I was so hungry, but my stomach was too weak to stand it. I suffered fearful pain for a day or two. I thought I should have died after all, but I pulled round again. I took a lot of killing! Another treat to me was a bit of good tobacco. How I enjoyed the first smoke. It made life worth living once more. At last Christmas 1917 came round. If it had not been for a parcel coming a day or so before, it would have been a very hungry Christmas for me as the Germans only provided the usual rubbish for meals.

On December 27th I was sent from Elbingerode, and after a 24 hours journey through Blankenburg, Halberstadt, Magdeburg, Ausburg and Hanover I landed at a place called Ronneberg. I found it was a salt mine. There were only French, Belgian and Russian prisoners there. The German Sergeant Major in charge took me for a Russian, in fact I must have looked like one. I had an old Russian coat on, a pair of old trousers miles too big for me, and on my feet wooden sabots, or clogs, stuffed with rags. I still had the trilby hat on, and my face was bloated out with water so much my eyes were like slits. All my worldly goods, my two thin blankets, bowl, spoon and an old tin or two that I boiled up in, along with the remains of my last parcels, were in an old sack slung over my shoulder. I

*December 1917 An almost fatal meal*

*December 1917 Sent to a Salt Mine*

must have looked a sight. I have seen tramps in England look a hundred times better than I looked.

I now could understand German. When I told the Sergeant Major I was English, he started cursing me, England and everything English. I admired his flow of language, as I was used to anything. I was sweinhund, or pig dog and a number of other endearing names. I thought what a nice quiet gentle creature this German is. He loves an Englishman according to the kindly welcome he is giving me. He turned to the guard who had come from Elbingerode with me, and said, "I don't want this thing". That meant me. I want Russians. These English pigs are stubborn and when you lick them into shape they die. I've had enough bother with English before. Russians don't matter no one makes a fuss over them dying. As I stood listening I thought, Tommy my boy, you've jumped out of the frying pan into the fire here. Then he turned to me and said, "Get off to the barrack there. I'll see what I can do with you in the morning."

The barracks was a big place built close to the pit. There was bunks built all round to the roof on landings. I picked up my traps and went in. In the bottom landing they were all Russian and Rumanian. I went up some steps to the next landing, these were Russians again. In the top I found Belgians and Frenchmen. I chucked my traps down, and sat on an empty bunk, tired and weary. The French and Belgians crowded round me talking in

*Marginal notes:*
December 1917
A Pleasant spoken German

German and some in English asking me what I was, where I came from, and how I had got in the state I was in. I told them what I had been through. They said poor chap and brought me biscuits and real coffee. They said I was not much better off there in the condition I was in as it was hard heavy work and long hours. Only strong healthy men could do it. They told me I was the only Englishman there, and I might get out of it by pleading the rule that no single nationality worked at those places alone.

I was lined up at 6am next morning on the pit bank along with the others. I was told by the Sergeant Major to get in the cage. I pleaded on what I had been told the night before, and that I was weak and ill. He cursed and raved, but I was fed up with everything, so I refused point blank to work, even if they killed me. The Sergeant Major waved his sword and the sentries pointed their rifles at me but I stood my ground. I did not care if they killed me. I could see if I stayed at that salt mine I should die in any case, so I thought I'll die now if I've got to die. Then the Major hit me in the face, and the next thing I remembered was one of my friends of the night before sponging my face with water in the barrack.

They told me I was to be sent to Hamlen the next day as it was the nearest prison camp. I got to Hamlen on December 31st 1917. I was put in a hut along with other prisoners who had come in that day. I was lying on the floor with my head throbbing as the New Year of 1918

December
31st
1917
I arrive at
Hamlen
Camp
came in, and I lay wondering what sort of luck it would bring me. The next day I saw the doctor. I was under his hands a month or six weeks. Never shall I forget the kindness of some British N.C.O.s. They had been in Hamlen since 1914. They said I was the worst case that had come in the camp since 1914. They went mad when I told them what I had been through. There were Sergeant Majors and Sergeants among them. I gave them the name and regiment of that devil in Elbingerode, and they sent an account to the General in Hanover asking for him to be punished, and the English who remained at Elbingerode to be brought to camp. I don't know whether that devil was punished, but all my old mates came in camp. They could not thank me enough for getting them out of that hell, but it was only by accident I had done it.

'I got my razor out that I had managed to buy.
I have got the same razor at home now.'

# 1918

I made especial friends with these 1914 Prisoners N.C.O.s. They had been getting their parcels from England regularly. They fed me, gave me clothes and a pair of boots. How nice it felt to have a good pair once more. At last my own parcels began to come through. I also had boots and clothes sent from England. I began to get strong again with the rest and the good food I was having now. I never ate the German stuff here. I had no need to do. I felt a different man. In February I was put on a job round the camp. This was with my pals asking the Kommandant for me to stay in the camp a bit, and telling him what I'd gone through, or I should have been sent out on another Kommando as soon as I was fit.

I enjoyed my stay here. On Sundays we did no work, and the prisoners would give theatrical performances in a hut fitted up as a theatre, and very good they were. I've got a programme of one yet. I very often went in the town of Hamlen in the course of my work. I had always a sentry with me when I went. It was a pretty old fashioned town on the river Wesser. It is noted for being the place of the Piper of Hamelin. On April 10th I was sent along with 19 more Englishmen on a Kommando.

After a 12 hours journey we landed at Munster in Hanover, a large soldiers' training centre. We were put in

January
1918
I arrive at
Munster

a small camp, with soldiers camps all round. In the camp we were put in they were mostly French and Belgian. Three Frenchmen and a Belgian were very kind to us here. With moving it upset the run of our parcels again, and they kept me and three of my pals in decent food until I got the parcels through again. I have a group photo of the eight of us taken together on a round stone seat.

May 1918
Work at
Kohlenbissen

Our work at Munster was in a big forest. The first month we were planting young fir trees. I have often wondered since if they have grown. After that we were put sawing trees down and trimming them. It was at a place called Kohlenbissen. It was about 4 miles from the camp. We used to start off at 6am. every morning and start back about 3pm. It was a good healthy job, and it was getting splendid weather, as we were on it well into the summer. The Guards over us were decent chaps, and had been to the front, so we had many a friendly chat with them.

July 1918
Life in
Munster
Camp

It was lovely walking through miles of forests with the birds singing in the morning, and as for food our parcels were coming regular now, so we did not eat what the Germans gave us. We gave it to the Russians. We also had every Sunday off to stroll about the camp or lie on our bunks. It was here I learned to read German. I was feeling now as fit as a fiddle and Elbingerode felt like a bad dream. There was a German soldiers punishment camp close to ours. We used to watch the poor devils drilling every night, after being out on hard work all day. Everything they did had to be done on the run, with a great pack on their backs. When they went out to work they had to run to it with their packs on. As they passed us most mornings, we used to slip cigarettes in their hands and bits of tobacco as they passed. It was worth something to see their grateful smile of thanks.

In another camp were soldiers training for the front. I have watched them at their drills many a time. The Germans were making their 1918 'Push on the Western Front' while I was here, and thousands of troops were coming to Munster and going out. When a big batch went out they were escorted by bands playing and banners flying. There also came to the hospital, close by to us, a big batch of wounded English prisoners taken in the push. They died in dozens. I was on burial parties every day. There was also the influenza raging. Every day when we came in from work we had to take coffins containing our countrymen to the cemetery. The coffins were just planks nailed together, and the bodies were put in stark naked. When we carried them shoulder high to the grave we could hear them rolling about in the coffins.

On the last day of August the tree chopping finished. I was then sent to Soltau Camp once more. On September 2nd after a night in what they called the louse hut, we went through the usual bath, hair cutting, and body shaving process. Then we were put in the main camp. It was rotten here. They took us out on all kinds of work every day, until, some nights, 9 and 10 o'clock. We were allowed no lights, and you had to get down in the dark, and if you had no parcels, you got no soup as you were too late -it was all gone by that time. Then there was not much chance of sleep for rats in dozens running over you, and fleas in millions biting you. On Sundays when you expected a day off like other camps, the sentries used to surround the huts to rush you off to work. I have jumped through the windows, and over fences, and been chased round the camp to get out of the way. When the sentry threatened to shoot, I've taken no notice, as I knew he was most likely to shoot one of his mates who were chasing other prisoners.

At last on September 18th I was sent on another Kommando with 3 other men. I landed at a place called
Ottersberg. We were sent to work on a hay pressing machine, but when we got there we found the machine had broken down. The German in charge said stay put for a few days, to see if I can get it repaired, as you don't know when you can get anything done while this war is on. I was there a week doing nothing. I wished I could have stayed there until the war was over. We slept in the boss's house. This was a village hotel.

We fed at the same table, and the beds were the same as they slept in, wooden four posters you sunk into, and a thick eiderdown quilt to cover you. The quilt was softer than anything I had slept on since I had been a soldier. We ate the same food as them. There was only his

September 1918 Too good to last

wife and daughter there, but he had a son at the war. We were treated like his own folk, at night the daughter would play the piano and we would sing for them. I was surprised to hear a lot of English songs in a German village. They had, 'Asleep in the Deep', 'After the Ball', 'Love me and the World is Mine' and many others. I sang them for the old German and his wife. We were treated as human beings once more. We were allowed to walk all round the village, and the village folk were friendly to us. I thought this was too good to last - and it was, the boss found out it would take months to get his machine put right.

September 1918 I arrive at Drentwede

They sent us then to another place called Drentwede, the other side of Bremen. We got here on September 23rd 1918. What a change here. No feather beds, and no walking round the village. It was a big saw mill, and the hut we slept in was just outside the saw shed. The hut was ringed all round by barbed wire. The only walk was to the latrines round the back. It was out of the hut at your work, finished work, back in your hut. It was like stabling horses after its days work. At night all our shoes were collected by the sentry on duty for the night. Two sentries slept at one end of the hut every night, while two more were on guard.

The hours of work here were 6 in the morning until 7 at night. After a while two of our mates were sent back to Soltau camp very ill. That only left another Englishman besides myself in the place. The other prisoners were French, Belgian, Italians and Russians, so we were a

October 1918
Work at Drentwede

mixed lot. Still I got on very well with them all. I got very friendly with a Russian Pole. He had found a way of dodging out, and he had a key to fit the store house of the German proprietor. He used to sneak bacon, eggs, bread, and all sorts of food, and I always had a share of it. The language we prisoners spoke to one another was German. We all understood that language. The work I did here was with a German on a machine that cut trees into planks.

October 1918
A German Worker

How that German worked. As fast as one tree came through, he would have another on the trolley following it up. He would start the machine as the buzzer blew 6am, and he never stopped until the buzzer had finished blowing for knocking off at dinner time. After dinner he stood against the starting wheel, to start it up at the first hoot of the buzzer. I used to curse him over it, but all he would say, smiling at my English and German curses getting mixed up, was "Englander Tom, I work for the Fatherland". He made me wild, he didn't seem to have a minute to breathe.

It was a humdrum life here. We were not badly treated. We had plenty of straw to lie on in the bunks. They put plenty of electric lights on, and I had one over my bunk that I could switch off or on as I lay in the bunk. I used to lie in my bunk reading anything I could get hold of half the night, and I was never interfered with over the electric light I used - they had their own plant for making power on the works. I got old newspapers given me by the German civvies and old books. I was called by the prisoners and

October
1918
Life at
Brentwede the sentries 'Tom the Reader'. The food here was the best I had had on a Kommando. It was still soup, but it was fairly good soup and did not make you shudder like the stuff I had had before. About October I read in the German papers that the Germans were after peace.

November
1918
Visions of
Home I had visions of going home again after 3 long years. I had almost given up hope of getting home again. At last about the 20th November I read in a paper dated the 12th that the Armistice had been signed on the 11th. The Germans had kept us in ignorance and kept us working. Among the terms I read was the immediate repatriation of Prisoners of War. I told my English mate and the others. We went almost mad with joy. We started singing and dancing and shaking hands with one another. The guards told us the Kaiser had fled to Holland, the country was in a tumult. I took the paper to the boss and showed him the terms about prisoners. "When are we going home?" He said "About another week". We kept on working until the Saturday, on the Sunday we had the day off. They let us walk round the village that day. I met the boss and I told him it was time we were being sent back to camp. He said, "I'll see on Monday". I did all the talking as my mate could not speak German. He was only a lad of 18 years old. He had only been captured in the May before.

On the Monday the guards called us up for work. I and my mate refused to get out. The others went out as usual, but the Russian Pole who was a pal, said as he went

November
1918
I go on
strike

out, "The Russians will stand by you". Not so the cowardly French and Belgians, all they said was, "Tom you will get half killed and the Germans will make you work still". I said "Rats to you". I could see the guards did not know what to do. They said "Get up and dress". I said to my mate, "Get up, we shall have a better chance dressed." The boss now came in, and he had a revolver in his hand. I said, "What have you got that for". He said it was to protect himself. He said, "You've infected the Russians, and they are standing about the place and won't work. I've sent for the Officer in charge of the district to see what he can do." He then said to us "Go to work, or when he comes he will make you". I sat on the bunk and said "No".

November
1918
A Rough
and
Tumble

At last the officer came with two more soldiers. He said, or rather roared, "Come get out to work". I said, "No, there is no more fighting, and we'll do no more work for Germany, and the Germans". That got their mad up. He said to the guards, "Into them, make them work". They went for us in a heap, foot and fist. My mate although, only 18, stuck to me like a true Briton, we lashed out right and left, and cleared a passage to the door. Then we made a bolt for it, with them after us, threatening to shoot.

November
1918
In the
clink

We were out of condition and they caught us in the village. Then they tore our clothes off and stripped our shoes off, and put us in a prison cell. Then they said, "You'll get no food, and you'll have a good hiding every day until you start work". We sat in the dark until about dinner time, then we heard someone at the keyhole. It was the Russian Pole. He said, "How are you going on, did they beat you?" I told him all, and he said, "We'll soon get you out of there".

He brought the rest of the Russians up, about 30 of them. They started to bash the doors in with iron bars. I heard the Pole say to the sentries, who came rushing up, "Keep back, we've all got knives - you'll only fire one shot, then you're done". They got us out and the guards gave us our clothes back. Then all the Russians said, "Send us back to camp with the Englishmen, we will not work any more". All this happened on November 25th 1918, 14 days after the armistice was signed. The officer came again and told the boss to send us to Soltau the next morning. The French and Belgians kept on working, they were too cowardly to strike. When the Russians asked them to help get us out of the cell, they said, "The English are not our comrades", but the Russians said, "They are ours and we will help them". We got no sleep that night we were singing and dancing with the Russians who had been such pals. They had melodeons and mouth organs. When I said, "We ought to go a bit quiet", they said, "Let's keep the French and Belgies awake, they've got to work in the morning!"

The next morning we were marched down to the station and they sent the sentries with us to take us to Soltau. So I bid adieu to Drentwede, and was on my way to Soltau Camp for the last time. When we got to Bremen we saw the German Sailors, who had ended the war by revolution. As I stood on the station waiting for a train to Soltau, they told us all about it. They wore red badges and red flags were hung all over the station.

November
1918
Arrive at
Soltau
At last we got to Soltau late in the afternoon of the 26th November. It was different than the last time I was here. No working parties, and you could roam about anywhere. The lights were put on in the huts, and were on all night so the rats did not trouble us. There was also plenty of food, as the parcels were dished out to everyone who came in the camp. We were told we had got to stay at Soltau until they could get a transport for us. At first we were alright, but as a week or two went by and no signs of moving we began to get restless. There were hundreds of prisoners. English, French, Belgian, Italians, Russians and Serbians in the camp, and more came in everyday. We were getting badly overcrowded. Then the 'flu broke out and some deaths took place. That put the wind up us. We all got together, about 1,800 English, and told the Germans we would march out in a body and make for Holland as we would rather drop on the road, than stay there to die of 'flu. If they tried to stop us, we would burn the camp down. This put the wind up the Germans. They wired to Berlin where some British Officers had arrived, stating the case. These Officers were dealing with the transport of British Prisoners, they wired back, "Start them off for Hamburg, we will get a ship there ready for them".

On Sunday morning December 22$^{nd}$ at about 4am we said our last goodbye to Soltau Prison Camp. There were no regrets in that good bye I can tell you. The train was brought up to the camp sidings. It was a long one with two engines. We got in and started on our last train journey in Germany. We were like a lot of school boys out for a holiday, singing and shouting and laughing, happy as could be at thoughts of going home again. We could hardly realise it to be true. I thought only 12 months ago I was being tortured at Elbingerode, and now I was on my way to England. It seemed too good to be true.

We got to Hamburg about 4pm and as the train steamed slowly into the docks there was a real British cheer from 1,800 throats. For there floating on a destroyer and a liner, was the Union Jack of Old England. The destroyer was steaming round the liner, the guns were pointing at the city and the blue jackets were waving a welcome to us. The liner was called the City of Poona. We had to be packed on as they only expected 1,000 men, and there were 1,800 of us. We were put on tables, on the decks in hammocks, in fact all the space was taken up, but we did not mind, we were going home again. We stayed at anchor that night. They allowed us to go on the destroyer to look round. It was a fine sight. Nothing but wheels, brass tubes and clocks, at least it seemed like that to me.

On Monday December 23rd 1918 we started for England. As I stood on deck and watched Hamburg fade out of sight I thought of what I had been through and I

December
1918 The
Voyage to
England

hoped I should never have to go through the same again in my life. In fact I do not think I could live through such a time again. We were sailing until the afternoon, when a violent storm came on. We had not been going very fast and were not far out of Hamburg. The ship had to anchor as it was not safe to go through the German minefield in such a storm.

December
1918
Anchored
in a Storm

As the darkness fell, we could see the destroyer that escorted us away on the left of us. There she was, great waves falling over her, and to us not used to the sea, we thought she would be sunk. She would climb up a big wave then down she seemed to dive, and another wave would rush onto her. When darkness fell we could see the lights of the destroyer as she circled round us. It was a fearful night. We went down below decks, and we could hear the waves dashing on the decks, and against the sides of the ship. It was just like thunder. We all had lifebelts on in case of a mine breaking loose, and striking the ship.

1918
Through
the
minefield

The storm died down again at daylight, as suddenly as it started. We had a German pilot in the ship. We were now going through the minefield. We were going zig zag, sometimes even backwards, the German pilot giving the directions all the time. We saw no end of mines floating about that had broken loose in the storm. They were like big round balls with spikes on them.

We got opposite Heligoland on Christmas Day 1918. Here the pilot left us in a motor launch that had brought his relief from Heligoland. The island was like a great red rock sticking out of the North Sea. They gave us a pipe and tobacco for Christmas and some pudding. It was strange to have Christmas in mid ocean. I had had Christmas in some places, the last four years. The next day we were getting close to dear old England. We climbed the masts and anywhere we could get to see the first sight of England. There were now ships of every description round us: warships, destroyers, submarines, steamers, and fishing smacks. When they saw our signal Repatriated Prisoners, it was like New Years Eve at home. They blew foghorns, buzzers and anything to let us know how they welcomed us home, and as we got close to Grimsby the buzzers on land took up the chorus. It was such a noise.

At last we got to Hull about 6pm on December 26th. We disembarked with crowds of folks cheering us, and shaking our hands. We were given a mug of tea, a sandwich and a bag of cakes by some ladies, the first English women I had seen since leaving Southampton. Then we were put in trains that were waiting and were off to Ripon. Outside the station at Ripon, a fleet of motor lorries and buses was waiting. We were taken to the camp. We got there about midnight. When we had been shown the huts where we were to sleep, we were taken to the dining hall. There we had the pleasure of having a good square meal. One that you used a knife and fork to - the first time I had needed a knife and fork for a year or two. In Germany a bowl and spoon was quite enough. How I enjoyed that feed, it was grand.

We stayed here resting the next day, as they said most of us looked as though we wanted a rest. We also were passed by the Doctor, he marked me C1, whatever that meant. On Saturday December 28th we were served out with 50/- each, to carry on with. I went down Ripon town at night, and went to the pictures. I had a shock when I went in a shop for some tobacco, and they charged me 8d an ounce, it was 3d when I left England. On the Sunday afternoon we were marched down to the railway station, and given a warrant to take us where we wanted to go. I got to Manchester about 7pm.

I got to Crewe about midnight. While waiting for a Stoke train to come in I met my brother in law Jack Clarke whom I had not seen for 4 years. He had been badly wounded in the arm. He came up to me and said, "Is that Higgins?" I said "Yes". We got in Hanley in the early hours of Monday December 30th 1918. I was pleased to get home once more to see my wife and youngster after three long years. "Be it ever so humble, there's no place like home".

I had a two month Prisoner of War leave with Army pay. At the end of that I went up to Lichfield on Friday March 1st 1919. After a night in barracks I was demobilised from the Army, dating March 31st, and came home to stop on the Saturday March 2nd.

So ended my life as a soldier in the British Army in the Great War.

# After the War

God and Soldiers men adore
In times of War, but not before
When War is over, and things are righted
God is forgotten and Soldiers are slighted

# 1914

Come you working men, leave your situations, your homes, your wives and children. Your King and Country need you. Go and fight for your Country. You will be looked after when you come back. We shall never see you want.

# 1919 to 1926 - Forgotten

Some of these men have returned to the country they fought for. Some will never return. They lie across the sea in graves close to the great battlefields. Have they died in vain. They say we have won the War. The men who have come back often wonder if it were not better to have died a soldier's death out yonder than to have come back and live in poverty in the land of the Brave and the Free.

Soldiers have come back to find the people who cheered us and gave us promises, are the same who try to give us starvation, give us lower wages and dear food. For those who need houses they are building them at 15/- a week. Add to this dear clothes and coal, and thousands unemployed. It makes you wonder who have come off best. Those who pulled through, or those who went west.

# Songs of the Trenches

These are a few of the songs we sung when on the march in France. Most of these went to the tunes of well-known hymns. Most battalions sang this to the tune of 'What a Friend we have in Jesus'. Each battalion altered the words but this was the best version.

Only just one more reveille,
Only one more night parade,
Only one more kit inspection,
Then we're marching home again,
When we get our civvies clothes on,
Oh how happy we shall be!
When this bloody war is over,
No more soldiering for me.
Complaints will then be fewer,
Guards, fatigues will be no more,
We'll be spooning with the wenches,
As we did in days of yore.
N.C.O.'s will then be navvies,
Privates own their motor cars,
No more "sir-ring", or saluting,
No more tea in two-pound jars.
No more "Smarter men, Now smarter!"
No more bread like granite rock
No more rising at five-thirty
Or "Lights Out", at ten o clock
No more asking when we're marching
"Please Sir, may we have a drink"
Or because we drop a shovel,
No more putting in the clink

No "Shun"-ing, and "as you were"-ing
No more working for a bob a day
When next the country has a war on
We'll find a job that brings more pay

Another song we sang at Monchy to the tune of 'Sing me to Sleep'.

Sing me to sleep, where bullets fall.
Let me forget, the world and all.
Damp is my dugout, wet are my feet.
Nothing but bully, and biscuits to eat.
Sing me to sleep, where bombs explode,
And shrapnel bullets, are in mode.
Over the sandbags, helmets you'll find,
Corpses in front and curses behind.
Far, far, from Monchy I want to be,
Where German snipers, can't get at me.
Think of me crouching, where the worms creep.
Waiting for someone to put me to sleep.

Then if we met the Army Service Corps on the roads with their motor lorries, we would burst out, to the tune of 'The Church's one Foundation', with the following parody:

We are Fed Karno's Army
We are the A.S.C.
We cannot shoot, we cannot fight
What earthly use are we.
And if we got to Berlin
The Kaiser, he will say
Hoch! Hoch! Mine Gott
What a damn fine lot
Are the British A.S.C.

One of the songs that we used to sing whenever we were paraded
to go up the line after we had been out a few days.

> I want to go home.
> I want to go home.
> I don't want to go in the trenches again
> The shrapnel and bullets,
> Are flying like rain.
> Take me home o'er the sea,
> Where Jerry can't get at me.
> "Oh my, I don't want to die.
> I want to go home.

Then after this complaint we should burst out with this:

> No rest for the 5th North Staffords,
> No rest for our Brigade,
> No rest for the 5th North Staffords,
> We're always on parade.
> Inspections, and Iron rations,
> And lectures on Gas bags too.
> Now we're off to the baths,
> To catch the little chats,
> And were off to the trenches in the evening.

The gem of the lot was the song we sung on the Somme in 1916,
as we marched to that inferno, so many of us never came back:

> The bells of hell go ting-a-ling
> For you, but not for me;
> For me the angels sing-a-ling;
> They've got the goods for me,
> Oh, death! Where is thy sting-a-ling?
> Oh, grave! Thy victory?
> The bells of hell go ting-a-ling
> For you but not for me.

# June 30th 1916

July 1st 1916, ten years ago , or to be exact the evening of the 30th June. The 5th North Staffs were at a place called Humbercamps, about three miles from the firing line. We were to march to Foncquevillers, where we held the front, to make an attack on the Germans who held the wood and the village of Gommecourt in front.

It was a beautiful evening and the Battalion stood on parade on a field, the sun was setting in a sea of red and gold. It was a scene I shall see in my memory if I live to be a very old man; and I've tried to convey it in a few poor verses, how it affected me; and affects me still whenever I hear that hymn sung even now. "God be with you 'til we meet again". I make no apology for the quality of the verses as I do not regard myself as a poet. I regard them as a tribute to my comrades who died that day for Old England.

> The years roll on, as life passes by,
> But still leave memories, that will not die.
> Until I go, as all men must,
> Beyond this vale is dust to dust.
>
> As I look back, o'er the years long fled,
> I see those alive, who now are dead.
> I see my old comrades, so brave and bold;
> Stand on parade, mid a sunset of gold.
>
> I can still see that scene, though ten years have sped,
> Hear our Colonel speak, and the words he said.
> Well Boys he cried; and his voice rang clear
> It is forward now, and have no fear.
> Tomorrow morn, if the luck holds good;
> I hope to be with you, in Gommecourt Wood.

Tommy at Gommecourt

And then there fell a silence,
Upon the evening air.
It seemed as though, eight hundred men
Were deep in silent prayer.

Thoughts of loved ones, in old England;
Brought many a tender sigh.
For every one of them knew well.
That some were bound to die.

Then once again was the silence broke,
As they sang a sweet refrain,
The hymn they sang; with heart and voice,
Was 'Til we meet again'.

Many of those who sang that song,
'Ere another day was done.
Had crossed into the "Great Beyond".
Their course on earth was run.

The Colonel who had made that speech,
Of where he hoped to be,
Is perhaps, still leading on his men
To immortality.

In the sunset glow the men stood there,
With visions before their eyes.
It seemed a prayer came from their hearts
And mounted to the skies

I always see that picture now.
When I hear that sweet refrain
Their voices echo these words to me,
'Til we meet again'.

T. Higgins

# November 23rd 1926

I went to the Capital to see the picture of Retreat from Mons. It was a fine picture. It showed you just a part of the dangers and sacrifices made during that terrible time. To see those British Soldiers undaunted by fearful odds dashing forward to face death at the call of old England. Then they said at the time, England will never forget.

As I sat watching that picture I could remember the times I have been in the same sort of scenes of death and destruction. Then I thought of the return we are getting today from a grateful country. On the 11th November the whole country did homage to those who had gone beyond. At the same time lots of us who went through those years of hell are out of work and on the dole. At the labour exchange you see the same men who dashed over to kill the Germans or be killed in the attempt themselves.

They are those same men but where is the fearlessness and dash, it is gone. They stand lined up in queues trembling in anticipation of having to face a committee composed of men who did not face the horrors of the war but skulked on munitions. These committees say whether a man's meagre dole shall continue or be stopped altogether. Not caring now if we live or die. Such is the England fit for Heroes.

And such is our reward from a grateful country. Living on the dole, out of work through the miner's strike and in dread and fear of being thrown off the dole any day. Was it worth fighting for? I don't think so.

# The Higgins Military Dynasty

Thomas James Higgins 1889-1968 was the first of four generations and 91 years of serving soldiers.

Thomas served in the 1/5th North Staffordshire Regiment, in the 1914-1918 war, and was awarded the Defence Medal and Victory Medal.

He worked at Shelton Iron and Steel Works, Stoke-on-Trent, for fifty years, including his wartime service.

Henry Higgins, 1919-1996, served in the Royal Artillery and the 2nd Airborne Brigade 1939-1946, and saw action at the battles of El Alamein and Monte Casino. He was awarded the Defence Medal, the Victory Medal, the 1939-1945 Star, the African Star, the Italy Star and the Territorial Long Service Medal.

He spent all his working life at the Shelton Iron and Steel Works.

Alan Henry Higgins served in the Grenadier Guards, 1960-1984, seeing action in Cyprus and Northern Ireland, and attaining the rank of WO1 (RSM). He was awarded the United Nations Forces in Cyprus Medal, the General Service Medal for Northern Ireland and the Long Service and Good Conduct Medal.

He went on to serve twenty years in Her Majesty's Prison Service at Stafford.

Alan David Higgins has served in the Grenadier Guards from 1985, seeing active service in Northern Ireland and Bosnia.

He has been so far awarded the General Service Medal for Northern Ireland, the Balkans Medal, the Golden Jubilee Medal, the Accumulated Service Medal, and the Long Service and Good Conduct Medal.

Thomas Higgins

Henry Higgins

The medals                            Alan Henry Higgins

Alan David Higgins in Bosnia

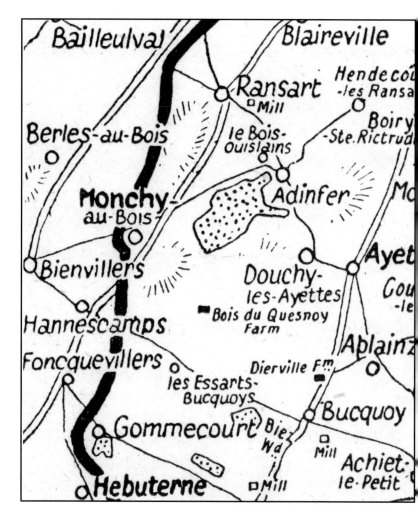

A contemporary map showing the area of Tommy Higgins' war